EDGAR ALLAN POE

Complete
Poems

EDGAR ALLAN POE

Complete Poems

GRAMERCY BOOKS
New York • Avenel, New Jersey

Introduction
Copyright © 1992 by Outlet Book Company, Inc.

This 1992 edition is published by Gramercy Books,
distributed by Outlet Book Company, Inc.,
a Random House Company,
40 Engelhard Avenue,
Avenel, New Jersey 07001.

Printed and bound in the United States

Library of Congress Cataloging-in-Publication Data
Poe, Edgar Allan, 1809–1849.
[Poems]
The complete poems of Edgar Allan Poe.
p. cm.
ISBN 0-517-08245-4
I. Title.
PS2605.A1 1992
811'.3—dc20   92-10200   CIP

8 7 6 5 4 3 2 1

CONTENTS

INTRODUCTION

Edgar Allan Poe's life was tragic and tormented. Not only was it short, but it was marked by almost unremitting misery and misfortune. The child of itinerant actors, Poe was born in Boston on January 19, 1809, the second of three children. Orphaned at an early age—both parents died of tuberculosis—he was adopted by Frances Allan, the childless wife of John Allan, a prosperous Richmond tobacco merchant. His childhood was relatively comfortable and stable; he was athletic and an excellent student with a promising future. In 1826, Poe entered the University of Virginia, but his excessive drinking and quarrels with his foster father about finances and his gambling debts forced him to leave after a year, whereupon he joined the army for two years. In 1830 he entered West Point, but left soon afterwards because of John Allan's continued lack of financial support.

Although Poe had published his first volume of verse, *Tamerlane and Other Poems*, in 1827, it gained little critical or popular notice. His literary career truly started some years later when he began to write short stories for magazines. He also worked for several important magazines where his outstanding skills as an editor and critic gained him some prominence and respect. But personal problems and poverty continued to plague him, and his alcoholism cost him several editorial posts. In 1836, Poe married his fourteen-year-old cousin, Virginia Clemm, but her ill health was a constant source of anxiety. Her death in 1847, of tuberculosis, led to Poe's complete mental and physical breakdown. When he recovered he joined a temperance society and became engaged to his childhood sweetheart, Elmira Royston Shelton. Then, on

October 3, 1849, he was found beaten and unconscious in an alley and was taken to a Baltimore charity hospital where he died four days later without ever regaining consciousness. The exact circumstances of his death will forever remain a mystery.

Part of the popular fascination with Poe is his image as a tortured genius. The novelist D.H. Lawrence said that Poe was "doomed to seethe down his soul in a great continuous convulsion of disintegration, and doomed to register the process." But this view undermines the full extent of Poe's brilliance and his enormous influence. The poet W.H. Auden said, "No one in his time, put so much energy and insight into making his contemporary poets take their craft seriously."

Poe is considered the father of the detective story and the modern gothic horror tale, as well as a great lyric poet. He was the first modern writer to explore the darker recesses of the human psyche in poems and stories, which seem to take place in the surreal landscapes and situations of nightmares. Although considered one of the great writers of short fiction, Poe had an affinity for verse. "With me, poetry has been not a purpose but a passion," he wrote. His poetry is rich with musical phrases and sensuous, evocative imagery. Poems like "The Raven," "The Bells," and "Annabel Lee," remain among the most popular and technically accomplished in the English language.

Collected in this volume are the complete poems of Edgar Allan Poe, arranged in reverse chronological order, except for the scenes from his play, "Politan," which are placed last. A constant editor of his own work, his final versions are used, except in the instances where an earlier version is of interest.

CHRISTOPHER MOORE

New York
1992

ANNABEL LEE

It was many and many a year ago,
    In a kingdom by the sea,
That a maiden there lived whom you may know
    By the name of Annabel Lee;—
And this maiden she lived with no other thought
    Than to love and be loved by me.

She was a child and *I* was a child,
    In this kingdom by the sea,
But we loved with a love that was more than love—
    I and my Annabel Lee—
With a love that the wingéd seraphs of Heaven
    Coveted her and me.

And this was the reason that, long ago,
    In this kingdom by the sea,
A wind blew out of a cloud by night
    Chilling my Annabel Lee;
So that her highborn kinsmen came
    And bore her away from me,
To shut her up in a sepulcher
    In this kingdom by the sea.

The angels, not half so happy in Heaven,
    Went envying her and me:—
Yes! that was the reason (as all men know,
    In this kingdom by the sea)
That the wind came out of a cloud, chilling
    And killing my Annabel Lee.

But our love it was stronger by far than the love
       Of those who were older than we—
       Of many far wiser than we—
And neither the angels in Heaven above
       Nor the demons down under the sea,
Can ever dissever my soul from the soul
       Of the beautiful Annabel Lee:—

For the moon never beams without bringing me
    dreams
       Of the beautiful Annabel Lee;
And the stars never rise but I see the bright eyes
       Of the beautiful Annabel Lee;
And so, all the nighttide, I lie down by the side
Of my darling, my darling, my life and my bride,
       In her sepulcher there by the sea—
       In her tomb by the side of the sea.

TO MY MOTHER

Because I feel that, in the heavens above,
   The angels, whispering to one another,
Can find, among their burning terms of love,
   None so devotional as that of "Mother,"
Therefore by that dear name I long have called you—
   You who are more than mother unto me,
And fill my heart of hearts, where Death installed you,
   In setting my Virginia's spirit free.
My mother—my own mother, who died early,
   Was but the mother of myself; but you
Are mother to the one I loved so dearly,
   And thus are dearer than the mother I knew
By that infinity with which my wife
   Was dearer to my soul than its soul-life.

ELDORADO

Gaily bedight,
A gallant knight,
In sunshine and in shadow,
Had journeyed long,
Singing a song,
In search of Eldorado.

But he grew old—
This knight so bold—
And o'er his heart a shadow
Fell as he found
No spot of ground
That looked like Eldorado.

And, as his strength
Failed him at length,
He met a pilgrim shadow—
"Shadow," said he,
"Where can it be—
This land of Eldorado?"

"Over the Mountains
Of the Moon,
Down the Valley of the Shadow,
Ride, boldly ride,"
The shade replied,—
"If you seek for Eldorado."

FOR ANNIE

Thank Heaven! the crisis—
    The danger is past,
And the lingering illness
    Is over at last—
And the fever called "Living"
    Is conquered at last.

Sadly, I know
    I am shorn of my strength,
And no muscle I move
    As I lie at full length—
But no matter!—I feel
    I am better at length.

And I rest so composedly
    Now, in my bed,
That any beholder
    Might fancy me dead—
Might start at beholding me,
    Thinking me dead.

The moaning and groaning,
    The sighing and sobbing,
Are quieted now,
    With that horrible throbbing
At heart:—ah that horrible,
    Horrible throbbing!

The sickness—the nausea—
    The pitiless pain—
Have ceased, with the fever
    That maddened my brain—
With the fever called "Living"
    That burned in my brain.

And oh! of all tortures
    That torture the worst
Has abated—the terrible
    Torture of thirst
For the napthaline river
    Of Passion accurst:—
I have drunk of a water
    That quenches all thirst:—

Of a water that flows,
    With a lullaby sound,
From a spring but a very few
    Feet under ground—
From a cavern not very far
    Down under ground.

And ah! let it never
    Be foolishly said
That my room it is gloomy
    And narrow my bed;
For man never slept
    In a different bed—
And, to *sleep*, you must slumber
    In just such a bed.

My tantalized spirit
  Here blandly reposes,
Forgetting, or never
  Regretting, its roses—
Its old agitations
  Of myrtles and roses:

For now, while so quietly
  Lying, it fancies
A holier odor
  About it, of pansies—
A rosemary odor,
  Commingled with pansies—
With rue and the beautiful
  Puritan pansies.

And so it lies happily,
  Bathing in many
A dream of the truth
  And the beauty of Annie—
Drowned in a bath
  Of the tresses of Annie.

She tenderly kissed me,
  She fondly caressed,
And then I fell gently
  To sleep on her breast—
Deeply to sleep
  From the heaven of her breast.

When the light was extinguished,
    She covered me warm,
And she prayed to the angels
    To keep me from harm—
To the queen of the angels
    To shield me from harm.

And I lie so composedly,
    Now, in my bed,
(Knowing her love)
    That you fancy me dead—
And I rest so contentedly,
    Now, in my bed,
(With her love at my breast)
    That you fancy me dead—
That you shudder to look at me,
    Thinking me dead: —

But my heart it is brighter
    Than all of the many
Stars of the sky,
    For it sparkles with Annie—
It glows with the light
    Of the love of my Annie—
With the thought of the light
    Of the eyes of my Annie.

TO HELEN

I saw thee once—once only—years ago:
I must not say *how* many—but *not* many.
It was a July midnight; and from out
A full-orbed moon, that, like thine own soul, soaring,
Sought a precipitate pathway up through heaven,
There fell a silvery-silken veil of light,
With quietude, and sultriness, and slumber,
Upon the upturn'd faces of a thousand
Roses that grew in an enchanted garden,
Where no wind dared to stir, unless on tiptoe—
Fell on the upturn'd faces of these roses
That gave out, in return for the love-light,
Their odorous souls in an ecstatic death—
Fell on the upturn'd faces of these roses
That smiled and died in this parterre, enchanted
By thee, and by the poetry of thy presence.

Clad all in white, upon a violet bank
I saw thee half reclining; while the moon
Fell on the upturn'd faces of the roses,
And on thine own, upturn'd—alas, in sorrow!

Was it not Fate, that, on this July midnight—
Was it not Fate, (whose name is also Sorrow),
That bade me pause before that garden gate,
To breathe the incense of those slumbering roses?
No footstep stirred: the hated world all slept,
Save only thee and me. (Oh, heaven!—oh, God!
How my heart beats in coupling those two words!)
Save only thee and me. I paused—I looked—
And in an instant all things disappeared.
(Ah, bear in mind this garden was enchanted!)

The pearly luster of the moon went out:
The mossy banks and the meandering paths,
The happy flowers and the repining trees,
Were seen no more: the very roses' odors
Died in the arms of the adoring airs.
All—all expired save thee—save less than thou:
Save only the divine light in thine eyes—
Save but the soul in thine uplifted eyes.
I saw but them—they were the world to me.
I saw but them—saw only them for hours—
Saw only them until the moon went down.
What wild heart-histories seemed to lie enwritten
Upon those crystalline, celestial spheres!
How dark a wo! yet how sublime a hope!
How silently serene a sea of pride!
How daring an ambition! yet how deep—
How fathomless a capacity for love!

But now, at length, dear Dian sank from sight,
Into a western couch of thundercloud;
And thou, a ghost, amid the entombing trees
Didst glide away. *Only thine eyes remained.*
They *would not* go—they never yet have gone.
Lighting my lonely pathway home that night,
They have not left me (as my hopes have) since.
They follow me—they lead me through the years
They are my ministers—yet I their slave.
Their office is to illumine and enkindle—
My duty, *to be saved* by their bright light,
And purified in their electric fire,
And sanctified in their elysian fire.
They fill my soul with Beauty (which is Hope),
And are far up in Heaven—the stars I kneel to
In the sad, silent watches of my night;
While even in the meridian glare of day
I see them still—two sweetly scintillant
Venuses, unextinguished by the sun!

A DREAM WITHIN A DREAM

Take this kiss upon the brow!
And, in parting from you now,
Thus much let me avow—
You are not wrong, who deem
That my days have been a dream;
Yet if Hope has flown away
In a night, or in a day,
In a vision, or in none,
Is it therefore the less *gone?*
All that we see or seem
Is but a dream within a dream.

I stand amid the roar
Of a surf-tormented shore,
And I hold within my hand
Grains of the golden sand—
How few! yet how they creep
Through my fingers to the deep,
While I weep—while I weep!
O God! can I not grasp
Them with a tighter clasp?
O God! can I not save
One from the pitiless wave?
Is *all* that we see or seem
But a dream within a dream?

THE BELLS

I

Hear the sledges with the bells—
Silver bells!
What a world of merriment their melody foretells!
How they tinkle, tinkle, tinkle,
In the icy air of night!
While the stars that oversprinkle
All the heavens, seem to twinkle
With a crystalline delight;
Keeping time, time, time,
In a sort of Runic rhyme,
To the tintinnabulation that so musically wells
From the bells, bells, bells, bells,
Bells, bells, bells—
From the jingling and the tinkling of the bells.

II

Hear the mellow wedding bells—
Golden bells!
What a world of happiness their harmony foretells!
Through the balmy air of night
How they ring out their delight!—
From the molten-golden notes,
And all in tune,
What a liquid ditty floats
To the turtledove that listens, while she gloats
On the moon!
Oh, from out the sounding cells,
What a gush of euphony voluminously wells!
How it swells!
How it dwells
On the Future!—how it tells

Of the rapture that impels
To the swinging and the ringing
Of the bells, bells, bells—
Of the bells, bells, bells, bells,
Bells, bells, bells—
To the rhyming and the chiming of the bells!

III

Hear the loud alarum bells—
Brazen bells!
What a tale of terror, now, their turbulency tells!
In the startled ear of night
How they scream out their affright!
Too much horrified to speak,
They can only shriek, shriek,
Out of tune,
In a clamorous appealing to the mercy of the fire,
In a mad expostulation with the deaf and frantic fire,
Leaping higher, higher, higher,
With a desperate desire,
And a resolute endeavor
Now—now to sit, or never,
By the side of the palefaced moon.
Oh, the bells, bells, bells!
What a tale their terror tells
Of Despair!
How they clang, and clash, and roar!
What a horror they outpour
On the bosom of the palpitating air!
Yet the ear, it fully knows,
By the twanging
And the clanging,
How the danger ebbs and flows;
Yet the ear distinctly tells,
In the jangling

And the wrangling,
How the danger sinks and swells,
By the sinking or the swelling in the anger of the bells—
Of the bells,—
Of the bells, bells, bells, bells,
Bells, bells, bells—
In the clamor and the clangor of the bells!

IV

Hear the tolling of the bells—
Iron bells!
What a world of solemn thought their monody compels!
In the silence of the night,
How we shiver with affright
At the melancholy menace of their tone!
For every sound that floats
From the rust within their throats
Is a groan.
And the people—ah, the people—
They that dwell up in the steeple,
All alone,
And who tolling, tolling, tolling,
In that muffled monotone,
Feel a glory in so rolling
On the human heart a stone—
They are neither man nor woman—
They are neither brute nor human—
They are Ghouls:—
And their king it is who tolls:—
And he rolls, rolls, rolls,
Rolls
A pæan from the bells!
And his merry bosom swells
With the pæan of the bells!
And he dances, and he yells;

Keeping time, time, time,
In a sort of Runic rhyme,
    To the pæan of the bells—
    Of the bells: —
Keeping time, time, time,
In a sort of Runic rhyme,
    To the throbbing of the bells—
  Of the bells, bells, bells—
    To the sobbing of the bells;
Keeping time, time, time,
  As he knells, knells, knells,
In a happy Runic rhyme,
    To the rolling of the bells—
  Of the bells, bells, bells: —
    To the tolling of the bells—
Of the bells, bells, bells, bells,
      Bells, bells, bells—
To the moaning and the groaning of the bells.

AN ENIGMA

"Seldom we find," says Solomon Don Dunce,
    "Half an idea in the profoundest sonnet.
Through all the flimsy things we see at once
    As easily as through a Naples bonnet—
    Trash of all trash!—how *can* a lady don it?
Yet heavier far than your Petrarchan stuff—
Owl-downy nonsense that the faintest puff
    Twirls into trunk paper the while you con it."
And, veritably, Sol is right enough.
The general tuckermanities are arrant
Bubbles—ephemeral and *so* transparent—
    But *this* is, now,—you may depend upon it—
Stable, opaque, immortal—all by dint
Of the dear names that lie concealed within 't.

ULALUME—A BALLAD

The skies they were ashen and sober;
    The leaves they were crispéd and sere—
    The leaves they were withering and sere:
It was night, in the lonesome October
    Of my most immemorial year:
It was hard by the dim lake of Auber,
    In the misty mid region of Weir—
It was down by the dank tarn of Auber,
    In the ghoul-haunted woodland of Weir.

Here once, through an alley Titanic,
    Of cypress, I roamed with my Soul—
    Of cypress, with Psyche, my Soul.
These were days when my heart was volcanic
    As the scoriac rivers that roll—
    As the lavas that restlessly roll
Their sulphurous currents down Yaanek
    In the ultimate climes of the Pole—
That groan as they roll down Mount Yaanek
    In the realms of the Boreal Pole.

Our talk had been serious and sober,
    But our thoughts they were palsied and sere—
    Our memories were treacherous and sere;
For we knew not the month was October,
    And we marked not the night of the year
    (Ah, night of all nights in the year!)—
We noted not the dim lake of Auber
    (Though once we had journeyed down here)—
We remembered not the dank tarn of Auber,
    Nor the ghoul-haunted woodland of Weir.

And now, as the night was senescent
    And star-dials pointed to morn—
    As the star-dials hinted of morn—
At the end of our path a liquescent
    And nebulous luster was born,
Out of which a miraculous crescent
    Arose with a duplicate horn—
Astarte's bediamonded crescent
    Distinct with its duplicate horn.

And I said: "She is warmer than Dian;
    She rolls through an ether of sighs—
    She revels in a region of sighs.
She has seen that the tears are not dry on
    These cheeks, where the worm never dies,
And has come past the stars of the Lion,
    To point us the path to the skies—
    To the Lethean peace of the skies—
    Come up, in despite of the Lion,
    To shine on us with her bright eyes—
Come up through the lair of the Lion,
    With love in her luminous eyes."

But Psyche, uplifting her finger,
    Said: "Sadly this star I mistrust—
    Her pallor I strangely mistrust:
Ah, hasten!—ah, let us not linger!
    Ah, fly!—let us fly!—for we must."
In terror she spoke, letting sink her
    Wings till they trailed in the dust—
In agony sobbed, letting sink her
    Plumes till they trailed in the dust—
    Till they sorrowfully trailed in the dust.

I replied: "This is nothing but dreaming:
 Let us on by this tremulous light!
 Let us bathe in this crystalline light!
Its Sibyllic splendor is beaming
 With Hope and in Beauty tonight:—
 See!—it flickers up the sky through the night!
Ah, we safely may trust to its gleaming,
 And be sure it will lead us aright—
We surely may trust to a gleaming,
 That cannot but guide us aright,
 Since it flickers up to Heaven through the night."

Thus I pacified Psyche and kissed her,
 And tempted her out of her gloom—
 And conquered her scruples and gloom;
And we passed to the end of the vista,
 But were stopped by the door of a tomb—
 By the door of a legended tomb;
And I said: "What is written, sweet sister,
 On the door of this legended tomb?"
 She replied: "Ulalume—Ulalume!—
 'T is the vault of thy lost Ulalume!"

Then my heart it grew ashen and sober
 As the leaves that were crispéd and sere—
 As the leaves that were withering and sere;
And I cried: "It was surely October
 On *this* very night of last year
 That I journeyed—I journeyed down here!—
 That I brought a dread burden down here—
 On this night of all nights in the year,
 Ah, what demon hath tempted me here?
Well I know, now, this dim lake of Auber—
 This misty mid region of Weir—
Well I know, now, this dank tarn of Auber,
 This ghoul-haunted woodland of Weir."

Said we, then—the two, then: "Ah, can it
   Have been that the woodlandish ghouls—
   The pitiful, the merciful ghouls—
To bar up our way and to ban it
   From the secret that lies in these wolds—
   From the thing that lies hidden in these wolds—
Have drawn up the specter of a planet
   From the limbo of lunary souls—
This sinfully scintillant planet
   From the Hell of the planetary souls?"

TO —— —— ——

Not long ago, the writer of these lines,
In the mad pride of intellectuality,
Maintained "the power of words"—denied that ever
A thought arose within the human brain
Beyond the utterance of the human tongue:
And now, as if in mockery of that boast,
Two words—two foreign soft dissyllables—
Italian tones, made only to be murmured
By angels dreaming in the moonlit "dew
That hangs like chains of pearl on Hermon hill,"—
Have stirred from out the abysses of his heart,
Unthought-like thoughts that are the souls of thought,
Richer, far wilder, far diviner visions
Than even the seraph harper, Israfel,
Who has "the sweetest voice of all God's creatures,"
Could hope to utter. And I! my spells are broken.
The pen falls powerless from my shivering hand.
With thy dear name as text, though bidden by thee,
I cannot write—I cannot speak or think—
Alas, I cannot feel; for 't is not feeling,
This standing motionless upon the golden
Threshold of the wide-open gate of dreams,
Gazing, entranced, adown the gorgeous vista,
And thrilling as I see, upon the right,
Upon the left, and all the way along,
Amid empurpled vapors, far away
To where the prospect terminates—*thee only.*

TO M. L. S——

Of all who hail thy presence as the morning—
Of all to whom thine absence is the night—
The blotting utterly from out high heaven
The sacred sun—of all who, weeping, bless thee
Hourly for hope—for life—ah! above all,
For the resurrection of deep-buried faith
In Truth, in Virtue, in Humanity—
Of all who, on Despair's unhallowed bed
Lying down to die, have suddenly arisen
At thy soft-murmured words, "Let there be light!"
At the soft-murmured words that were fulfilled
In the seraphic glancing of thine eyes—
Of all who owe thee most, whose gratitude
Nearest resembles worship—oh, remember
The truest—the most fervently devoted,
And think that these weak lines are written by him—
By him, who, as he pens them, thrills to think
His spirit is communing with an angel's.

A VALENTINE

[To translate the address, read the first letter of the first line in connection with the second letter of the second line, the third letter of the third line, the fourth of the fourth, and so on to the end. The name will thus appear.]

For her this rhyme is penned, whose luminous eyes,
  Brightly expressive as the twins of Lœda,
Shall find her own sweet name, that, nestling lies
  Upon the page, enwrapped from every reader.
Search narrowly the lines!—they hold a treasure
  Divine—a talisman—an amulet
That must be worn *at heart*. Search well the measure—
  The words—the syllables! Do not forget
The trivialest point, or you may lose your labor!
  And yet there is in this no Gordian knot
Which one might not undo without a saber,
  If one could merely comprehend the plot.
Enwritten upon the leaf where now are peering
  Eyes scintillating soul, there lie *perdus*
Three eloquent words oft uttered in the hearing
  Of poets, by poets—as the name is a poet's too.
Its letters, although naturally lying
  Like the knight Pinto—Mendez Ferdinando—
Still form a synonym for Truth.—Cease trying!
  You will not read the riddle, though you do the best
  you *can* do.

THE RAVEN

Once upon a midnight dreary, while I pondered, weak
and weary,
Over many a quaint and curious volume of forgotten lore—
While I nodded, nearly napping, suddenly there came a
tapping,
As of some one gently rapping, rapping at my chamber
door.
" 'Tis some visitor," I muttered, "tapping at my chamber
door—
  Only this and nothing more."

Ah, distinctly I remember it was in the bleak December;
And each separate dying ember wrought its ghost upon the
floor.
Eagerly I wished the morrow;—vainly I had sought to
borrow
From my books surcease of sorrow—sorrow for the lost
Lenore—
For the rare and radiant maiden whom the angels name
Lenore—
  Nameless *here* for evermore.

And the silken, sad, uncertain rustling of each purple curtain
Thrilled me—filled me with fantastic terrors never felt
before;
So that now, to still the beating of my heart, I stood
repeating
" 'Tis some visiter entreating entrance at my chamber
door—
Some late visiter entreating entrance at my chamber
door;—
  This it is and nothing more."

Presently my soul grew stronger; hesitating then no longer,
"Sir," said I, "or Madam, truly your forgiveness I implore;
But the fact is I was napping, and so gently you came
    rapping,
And so faintly you came tapping, tapping at my chamber
    door,
That I scarce was sure I heard you"—here I opened wide
    the door;——
        Darkness there and nothing more.

Deep into that darkness peering, long I stood there
    wondering, fearing,
Doubting, dreaming dreams no mortal ever dared to dream
    before;
But the silence was unbroken, and the stillness gave no
    token,
And the only word there spoken was the whispered word,
    "Lenore?"
This I whispered, and an echo murmured back the word,
    "Lenore!"
        Merely this and nothing more.

Back into the chamber turning, all my soul within me
    burning,
Soon again I heard a tapping somewhat louder than before.
"Surely," said I, "surely that is something at my window
    lattice;
Let me see, then, what thereat is, and this mystery
    explore—
Let my heart be still a moment and this mystery explore;—
        'Tis the wind and nothing more!"

Open here I flung the shutter, when, with many a flirt and
  flutter,
In there stepped a stately Raven of the saintly days of yore;
Not the least obeisance made he; not a minute stopped or
  stayed he;
But, with mien of lord or lady, perched above my chamber
  door—
Perched upon a bust of Pallas just above my chamber door—
    Perched, and sat, and nothing more.

Then this ebony bird beguiling my sad fancy into smiling,
By the grave and stern decorum of the countenance it wore,
"Though thy crest be shorn and shaven, thou," I said, "art
  sure no craven,
Ghastly grim and ancient Raven wandering from the Nightly
  shore—
Tell me what thy lordly name is on the Night's Plutonian
  shore!"
    Quoth the Raven "Nevermore."

Much I marvelled this ungainly fowl to hear discourse so
  plainly,
Though its answer little meaning—little relevancy bore;
For we cannot help agreeing that no living human being
Ever yet was blessed with seeing bird above his chamber
  door—
Bird or beast upon the sculptured bust above his chamber
  door,
    With such name as "Nevermore."

But the Raven, sitting lonely on the placid bust, spoke only
That one word, as if his soul in that one word he did
  outpour.

Nothing farther then he uttered—not a feather then he
   fluttered—
Till I scarcely more than muttered "Other friends have flown
   before—
On the morrow *he* will leave me, as my Hopes have flown
   before."
      Then the bird said "Nevermore."

Startled at the stillness broken by reply so aptly spoken,
"Doubtless," said I, "what it utters is its only stock and store
Caught from some unhappy master whom unmerciful Disaster
Followed fast and followed faster till his songs one burden
   bore—
Till the dirges of his Hope that melancholy burden bore
      Of 'Never—nevermore.' "

But the Raven still beguiling my sad fancy into smiling,
Straight I wheeled a cushioned seat in front of bird, and
   bust and door;
Then, upon the velvet sinking, I betook myself to linking
Fancy unto fancy, thinking what this ominous bird of yore—
What this grim, ungainly, ghastly, gaunt, and ominous bird
   of yore
      Meant in croaking "Nevermore."

This I sat engaged in guessing, but no syllable expressing
To the fowl whose fiery eyes now burned into my bosom's
   core;
This and more I sat divining, with my head at ease reclining
On the cushion's velvet lining that the lamplight gloated o'er,
But whose velvet-violet lining with the lamplight gloating o'er,
      She shall press, ah, nevermore!

Then, methought, the air grew denser, perfumed from an
    unseen censer
Swung by seraphim whose footfalls tinkled on the tufted
    floor.
"Wretch," I cried, "thy God hath lent thee—by these
    angels he hath sent thee
Respite—respite and nepenthe from thy memories of
    Lenore;
Quaff, oh quaff this kind nepenthe and forget this lost
    Lenore!"
        Quoth the Raven "Nevermore."

"Prophet!" said I, "thing of evil!—prophet still, if bird or
    devil!—
Whether Tempter sent, or whether tempest tossed thee here
    ashore,
Desolate yet all undaunted, on this desert land enchanted—
On this home by Horror haunted—tell me truly, I
    implore—
Is there—*is* there balm in Gilead?—tell me—tell me, I
    implore!"
        Quoth the Raven "Nevermore."

"Prophet!" said I, "thing of evil!—prophet still, if bird or
    devil!
By that Heaven that bends above us—by that God we both
    adore—
Tell this soul with sorrow laden if, within the distant
    Aidenn,
It shall clasp a sainted maiden whom the angels name
    Lenore—
Clasp a rare and radiant maiden whom the angels name
    Lenore."
        Quoth the Raven "Nevermore."

"Be that word our sign of parting, bird or fiend!" I shrieked,
   upstarting—
"Get thee back into the tempest and the Night's Plutonian
   shore!
Leave no black plume as a token of that lie thy soul hath
   spoken!
Leave my loneliness unbroken!—quit the bust above my
   door!
Take thy beak from out my heart, and take thy form from
   off my door!"
      Quoth the Raven "Nevermore."

And the Raven, never flitting, still is sitting, *still* is sitting
On the pallid bust of Pallas just above my chamber door;
And his eyes have all the seeming of a demon's that is
   dreaming,
And the lamplight o'er him streaming throws his shadow
   on the floor;
And my soul from out that shadow that lies floating on the
   floor
      Shall be lifted—nevermore!

EULALIE—A SONG

I dwelt alone
In a world of moan,
And my soul was a stagnant tide,
Till the fair and gentle Eulalie became my blushing bride—
Till the yellow-haired young Eulalie became my smiling bride.

Ah, less—less bright
The stars of the night
Than the eyes of the radiant girl!
And never a flake
That the vapor can make
With the moon-tints of purple and pearl,
Can vie with the modest Eulalie's most unregarded
curl—
Can compare with the bright-eyed Eulalie's most humble
and careless curl.

Now Doubt—now Pain
Come never again,
For her soul gives me sigh for sigh,
And all day long
Shines, bright and strong,
Astarté within the sky,
While ever to her dear Eulalie upturns her matron eye—
While ever to her young Eulalie upturns her violet eye.

DREAMLAND

By a route obscure and lonely,
Haunted by ill angels only,
Where an Eidolon, named NIGHT,
On a black throne reigns upright,
I have reached these lands but newly
From an ultimate dim Thule—
From a wild weird clime that lieth, sublime,
    Out of SPACE—out of TIME.

Bottomless vales and boundless floods,
And chasms, and caves, and Titan woods,
With forms that no man can discover
For the tears that drip all over;
Mountains toppling evermore
Into seas without a shore;
Seas that restlessly aspire,
Surging, unto skies of fire;
Lakes that endlessly outspread
Their lone waters—lone and dead,—
Their still waters—still and chilly
With the snows of the lolling lily.

By the lakes that thus outspread
Their lone waters, lone and dead,—
Their sad waters, sad and chilly
With the snows of the lolling lily,—
By the mountains—near the river
Murmuring lowly, murmuring ever,—
By the gray woods,—by the swamp
Where the toad and the newt encamp,—
By the dismal tarns and pools
    Where dwell the Ghouls,—
By each spot the most unholy—

In each nook most melancholy,—
There the traveller meets, aghast,
Sheeted Memories of the Past—
Shrouded forms that start and sigh
As they pass the wanderer by—
White-robed forms of friends long given,
In agony, to the Earth—and Heaven.

For the heart whose woes are legion
'T is a peaceful, soothing region—
For the spirit that walks in shadow
'T is—oh 't is an Eldorado!
But the traveller, travelling through it,
May not—dare not openly view it;
Never its mysteries are exposed
To the weak human eye unclosed;
So wills its King, who hath forbid
The uplifting of the fringéd lid;
And thus the sad Soul that here passes
Beholds it but through darkened glasses.

By a route obscure and lonely,
Haunted by ill angels only,
Where an Eidolon, named NIGHT,
On a black throne reigns upright,
I have wandered home but newly
From this ultimate dim Thule.

THE CONQUEROR WORM

Lo! 't is a gala night
  Within the lonesome latter years!
An angel throng, bewinged, bedight
  In veils, and drowned in tears,
Sit in a theater, to see
  A play of hopes and fears,
While the orchestra breathes fitfully
  The music of the spheres.

Mimes, in the form of God on high,
  Mutter and mumble low,
And hither and thither fly—
  Mere puppets they, who come and go
At bidding of vast formless things
  That shift the scenery to and fro,
Flapping from out their Condor wings
  Invisible Woe!

That motley drama—oh, be sure
  It shall not be forgot!
With its Phantom chased for evermore,
  By a crowd that seize it not,
Through a circle that ever returneth in
  To the selfsame spot,
And much of Madness, and more of Sin,
  And Horror the soul of the plot.

But see, amid the mimic rout
  A crawling shape intrude!
A blood-red thing that writhes from out
  The scenic solitude!

It writhes!—it writhes!—with mortal pangs
  The mimes become its food,
And the angels sob at vermin fangs
  In human gore imbued.

Out—out are the lights—out all!
  And, over each quivering form,
The curtain, a funeral pall,
  Comes down with the rush of a storm,
And the angels, all pallid and wan,
  Uprising, unveiling, affirm
That the play is the tragedy "Man,"
  And its hero the Conqueror Worm.

SONNET — SILENCE

There are some qualities—some incorporate things,
   That have a double life, which thus is made
A type of that twin entity which springs
   From matter and light, evinced in solid and shade.
There is a twofold *Silence*—sea and shore—
   Body and soul. One dwells in lonely places,
   Newly with grass o'ergrown; some solemn graces,
Some human memories and tearful lore,
Render him terrorless: his name's "No More."
He is the corporate Silence: dread him not!
   No power hath he of evil in himself;
But should some urgent fate (untimely lot!)
   Bring thee to meet his shadow (nameless elf,
That haunteth the lone regions where hath trod
No foot of man,) commend thyself to God!

THE HAUNTED PALACE

In the greenest of our valleys
  By good angels tenanted,
Once a fair and stately palace—
  Radiant palace—reared its head.
In the monarch Thought's dominion—
  It stood there!
Never seraph spread a pinion
  Over fabric half so fair!

Banners yellow, glorious, golden,
  On its roof did float and flow,
(This—all this—was in the olden
  Time long ago,)
And every gentle air that dallied,
  In that sweet day,
Along the ramparts plumed and pallid,
  A wingéd odor went away.

Wanderers in that happy valley,
  Through two luminous windows, saw
Spirits moving musically,
  To a lute's well-tunéd law,
Round about a throne where, sitting
  (Porphyrogene!)
In state his glory well befitting,
  The ruler of the realm was seen.

And all with pearl and ruby glowing
   Was the fair palace door,
Through which came flowing, flowing, flowing,
   And sparkling evermore,
A troop of Echoes, whose sweet duty
   Was but to sing,
In voices of surpassing beauty,
   The wit and wisdom of their king.

But evil things, in robes of sorrow,
   Assailed the monarch's high estate.
(Ah, let us mourn!—for never morrow
   Shall dawn upon him, desolate!)
And round about his home the glory
   That blushed and bloomed,
Is but a dim-remembered story
   Of the old time entombed.

And travellers, now, within that valley,
   Through the red-litten windows see
Vast forms that move fantastically
   To a discordant melody,
While, like a ghastly rapid river,
   Through the pale door
A hideous throng rush out forever
   And laugh—but smile no more.

BRIDAL BALLAD

The ring is on my hand,
  And the wreath is on my brow;
Satins and jewels grand
Are all at my command,
  And I am happy now.

And my lord he loves me well;
  But, when first he breathed his vow,
I felt my bosom swell—
For the words rang as a knell,
And the voice seemed *his* who fell
In the battle down the dell,
  And who is happy now.

But he spoke to reassure me,
  And he kissed my pallid brow,
While a reverie came o'er me,
And to the churchyard bore me,
And I sighed to him before me,
(Thinking him dead D'Elormie),
  "Oh, I am happy now!"

And thus the words were spoken;
  And this the plighted vow;
And, though my faith be broken,
And, though my heart be broken,
Behold the golden token
  That *proves* me happy now!

Would God I could awaken!
     For I dream I know not how,
And my soul is sorely shaken
Lest an evil step be taken,—
Lest the dead who is forsaken
     May not be happy now.

SONNET—TO ZANTE

Fair isle, that from the fairest of all flowers,
     Thy gentlest of all gentle names dost take!
How many memories of what radiant hours
     At sight of thee and thine at once awake!
How many scenes of what departed bliss!
     How many thoughts of what entombéd hopes!
How many visions of a maiden that is
     No more—no more upon thy verdant slopes!
No more! alas, that magical sad sound
     Transforming all! Thy charms shall please *no*
          more—
Thy memory *no more!* Acc#ursed ground
     Henceforth I hold thy flower-enamelled shore,
O hyacinthine isle! O purple Zante!
     "Isola d'oro! Fior di Levante!"

TO F——S S. O——D

Thou wouldst be loved?—then let thy heart
   From its present pathway part not!
Being everything which now thou art,
   Be nothing which thou art not.
So with the world thy gentle ways,
   Thy grace, thy more than beauty,
Shall be an endless theme of praise,
   And love—a simple duty.

TO F——

Beloved! amid the earnest woes
   That crowd around my earthly path—
(Drear path, alas! where grows
Not even one lonely rose)—
   My soul at least a solace hath
In dreams of thee, and therein knows
An Eden of bland repose.

And thus thy memory is to me
   Like some enchanted far-off isle
In some tumultuous sea—
Some ocean throbbing far and free
   With storms—but where meanwhile
Serenest skies continually
   Just o'er that one bright island smile.

THE COLISEUM

Type of the antique Rome! Rich reliquary
Of lofty contemplation left to Time
By buried centuries of pomp and power!
At length—at length—after so many days
Of weary pilgrimage and burning thirst,
(Thirst for the springs of lore that in thee lie,)
I kneel, an altered and an humble man,
Amid thy shadows, and so drink within
My very soul thy grandeur, gloom, and glory!

Vastness! and Age! and Memories of Eld!
Silence! and Desolation! and dim Night!
I feel ye now—I feel ye in your strength—
O spells more sure than e'er Judæan king
Taught in the gardens of Gethsemane!
O charms more potent than the rapt Chaldee
Ever drew down from out the quiet stars!

Here, where a hero fell, a column falls!
Here, where the mimic eagle glared in gold,
A midnight vigil holds the swarthy bat!
Here, where the dames of Rome their gilded hair
Waved to the wind, now wave the reed and thistle!
Here, where on golden throne the monarch lolled,
Glides, specter-like, unto his marble home,
Lit by the wan light of the hornéd moon,
The swift and silent lizard of the stones!

But stay! these walls—these ivy-clad arcades—
These moldering plinths—these sad and blackened shafts—
These vague entablatures—this crumbling frieze—
These shattered cornices—this wreck—this ruin—

These stones—alas! these gray stones—are they all—
All of the famed, and the colossal left
By the corrosive Hours to Fate and me?

"Not all"—the Echoes answer me—"not all!
Prophetic sounds and loud, arise forever
From us, and from all Ruin, unto the wise,
As melody from Memnon to the Sun.
We rule the hearts of mightiest men—we rule
With a despotic sway all giant minds.
We are not impotent—we pallid stones.
Not all our power is gone—not all our fame—
Not all the magic of our high renown—
Not all the wonder that encircles us—
Not all the mysteries that in us lie—
Not all the memories that hang upon
And cling around about us as a garment,
Clothing us in a robe of more than glory."

SERENADE

So sweet the hour, so calm the time,
I feel it more than half a crime,
When Nature sleeps and stars are mute,
To mar the silence ev'n with lute.
At rest on ocean's brilliant dyes
An image of Elysium lies:
Seven Pleiades entranced in Heaven,
Form in the deep another seven:
Endymion nodding from above
Sees in the sea a second love.
Within the valleys dim and brown,
And on the spectral mountain's crown,
The wearied light is dying down,
And earth, and stars, and sea, and sky
Are redolent of sleep, as I
Am redolent of thee and thine
Enthralling love, my Adeline.
But list, O list,—so soft and low
Thy lover's voice tonight shall flow,
That, scarce awake, thy soul shall deem
My words the music of a dream.
Thus, while no single sound too rude
Upon thy slumber shall intrude,
Our thoughts, our souls—O God above!
In every deed shall mingle, love.

LENORE

Ah, broken is the golden bowl! the spirit flown forever!
Let the bell toll!—a saintly soul floats on the Stygian river:—
And, Guy De Vere, hast *thou* no tear?—weep now or never
    more!
See! on yon drear and rigid bier low lies thy love, Lenore!
Come! let the burial rite be read—the funeral song be sung!—
An anthem for the queenliest dead that ever died so young—
A dirge for her the doubly dead in that she died so young.

"Wretches! ye loved her for her wealth and hated her for her
    pride,
And, when she fell in feeble health, ye blessed her—that she
    died!
How *shall* the ritual, then, be read?—the requiem how be sung
By you—by yours, the evil eye,—by yours, the slanderous tongu
That did to death the innocence that died, and died so young?"

Peccavimus; but rave not thus! and let a Sabbath song
Go up to God so solemnly the dead may feel no wrong!
The sweet Lenore hath "gone before," with Hope, that flew
    beside,
Leaving thee wild for the dear child that should have been thy
    bride—
For her, the fair and *debonair*, that now so lowly lies,
The life upon her yellow hair but not within her eyes—
The life still there, upon her hair—the death upon her eyes.

"Avaunt!—avaunt! to friends from fiends the indignant ghost is riven—
From Hell unto a high estate within the utmost Heaven—
From moan and groan to a golden throne beside the King of Heaven:—
Let *no* bell toll, then, lest her soul, amid its hallowed mirth
Should catch the note as it doth float up from the damnéd Earth!
And I—tonight my heart is light:—no dirge will I upraise,
But waft the angel on her flight with a Pæan of old days!"

HYMN

At morn—at noon—at twilight dim—
Maria! thou hast heard my hymn!
In joy and woe—in good and ill—
Mother of God, be with me still!
When the Hours flew brightly by,
And not a cloud obscured the sky,
My soul, lest it should truant be,
Thy grace did guide to thine and thee;
Now, when storms of Fate o'ercast
Darkly my Present and my Past,
Let my Future radiant shine
With sweet hopes of thee and thine!

TO ONE IN PARADISE

Thou wast that all to me, love,
    For which my soul did pine—
A green isle in the sea, love,
    A fountain and a shrine,
All wreathed with fairy fruits and flowers
    And all the flowers were mine.

Ah, dream too bright to last!
    Ah, starry Hope! that didst arise
But to be overcast!
    A voice from out the Future cries,
"On! on!"—but o'er the Past
    (Dim gulf!) my spirit hovering lies
Mute, motionless, aghast!

For, alas! alas! with me
    The light of Life is o'er!
    "No more—no more—no more—"
(Such language holds the solemn sea
    To the sands upon the shore)
Shall bloom the thunder-blasted tree,
    Or the stricken eagle soar!

And all my days are trances,
    And all my nightly dreams
Are where thy dark eye glances,
    And where thy footstep gleams—
In what ethereal dances,
    By what eternal streams.

THE CITY IN THE SEA

Lo! Death has reared himself a throne
In a strange city lying alone
Far down within the dim West,
Where the good and the bad and the worst and the best
Have gone to their eternal rest.
There shrines and palaces and towers
(Time-eaten towers that tremble not!)
Resemble nothing that is ours.
Around, by lifting winds forgot,
Resignedly beneath the sky
The melancholy waters lie.

No rays from the holy heaven come down
On the long nighttime of that town;
But light from out the lurid sea
Streams up the turrets silently—
Gleams up the pinnacles far and free—
Up domes—up spires—up kingly halls—
Up fanes—up Babylon-like walls—
Up shadowy long-forgotten bowers
Of sculptured ivy and stone flowers—
Up many and many a marvellous shrine
Whose wreathéd friezes intertwine
The viol, the violet, and the vine.

Resignedly beneath the sky
The melancholy waters lie.
So blend the turrets and shadows there
That all seem pendulous in air,
While from a proud tower in the town
Death looks gigantically down.

There open fanes and gaping graves
Yawn level with the luminous waves;
But not the riches there that lie
In each idol's diamond eye—
Not the gaily-jewelled dead
Tempt the waters from their bed;
For no ripples curl, alas!
Along that wilderness of glass—
No swellings tell that winds may be
Upon some far-off happier sea—
No heavings hint that winds have been
On seas less hideously serene.

But lo, a stir is in the air!
The wave—there is a movement there!
As if the towers had thrust aside,
In slightly sinking, the dull tide—
As if their tops had feebly given
A void within the filmy Heaven.
The waves have now a redder glow—
The hours are breathing faint and low—
And when, amid no earthly moans,
Down, down that town shall settle hence,
Hell, rising from a thousand thrones,
Shall do it reverence.

THE VALLEY OF UNREST

Once it smiled a silent dell
Where the people did not dwell;
They had gone unto the wars,
Trusting to the mild-eyed stars,
Nightly, from their azure towers,
To keep watch above the flowers,
In the midst of which all day
The red sunlight lazily lay.
Now each visiter shall confess
The sad valley's restlessness.
Nothing there is motionless—
Nothing save the airs that brood
Over the magic solitude.
Ah, by no wind are stirred those trees
That palpitate like the chill seas
Around the misty Hebrides!
Ah, by no wind those clouds are driven
That rustle through the unquiet Heaven
Uneasily, from morn till even,
Over the violets there that lie
In myriad types of the human eye—
Over the lilies there that wave
And weep above a nameless grave!
They wave:—from out their fragrant tops
Eternal dews come down in drops.
They weep:—from off their delicate stems
Perennial tears descend in gems.

THE SLEEPER

At midnight, in the month of June,
I stand beneath the mystic moon.
An opiate vapor, dewy, dim,
Exhales from out her golden rim,
And, softly dripping, drop by drop,
Upon the quiet mountain top,
Steals drowsily and musically
Into the universal valley.
The rosemary nods upon the grave;
The lily lolls upon the wave;
Wrapping the fog about its breast,
The ruin molders into rest;
Looking like Lethe, see! the lake
A conscious slumber seems to take,
And would not, for the world, awake.
All Beauty sleeps!—and lo! where lies
Irene, with her Destinies!

Oh, lady bright! can it be right—
This window open to the night?
The wanton airs, from the treetop,
Laughingly through the lattice drop—
The bodiless airs, a wizard rout,
Flit through thy chamber in and out,
And wave the curtain canopy
So fitfully—so fearfully—
Above the closed and fringéd lid
'Neath which thy slumb'ring soul lies hid,
That, o'er the floor and down the wall,
Like ghosts the shadows rise and fall!

Oh, lady dear, hast thou no fear?
Why and what are thou dreaming here?
Sure thou art come o'er far-off seas,
A wonder to these garden trees!
Strange is thy pallor! strange thy dress!
Strange, above all, thy length of tress,
And this all solemn silentness!

The lady sleeps! Oh, may her sleep,
Which is enduring, so be deep!
Heaven have her in its sacred keep!
This chamber changed for one more holy,
This bed for one more melancholy,
I pray to God that she may lie
Forever with unopened eye,
While the pale sheeted ghosts go by!

My love, she sleeps! Oh, may her sleep,
As it is lasting, so be deep!
Soft may the worms about her creep!
Far in the forest, dim and old,
For her may some tall vault unfold—
Some vault that oft hath flung its black
And wingéd panels fluttering back,
Triumphant, o'er the crested palls,
Of her grand family funerals—
Some sepulcher, remote, alone,
Against whose portal she hath thrown,
In childhood, many an idle stone—
Some tomb from out whose sounding door
She ne'er shall force an echo more,
Thrilling to think, poor child of sin!
It was the dead who groaned within.

ISRAFEL

In Heaven a spirit doth dwell
  "Whose heartstrings are a lute;"
None sing so wildly well
As the angel Israfel,
And the giddy stars (so legends tell)
Ceasing their hymns, attend the spell
  Of his voice, all mute.

Tottering above
  In her highest noon,
  The enamored moon
Blushes with love,
  While, to listen, the red levin
  (With the rapid Pleiads, even,
  Which were seven,)
  Pauses in Heaven.

And they say (the starry choir
  And the other listening things)
That Israfeli's fire
Is owing to that lyre
  By which he sits and sings—
The trembling living wire
Of those unusual strings.

But the skies that angel trod,
  Where deep thoughts are a duty—
Where Love's a grown-up God—
  Where the Houri glances are
Imbued with all the beauty
  Which we worship in a star.

Therefore, thou art not wrong,
  Israfeli, who despisest
An unimpassioned song;
To thee the laurels belong,
  Best bard, because the wisest!
Merrily live, and long!

The ecstasies above
  With thy burning measure suit—
Thy grief, thy joy, thy hate, thy love,
  With the fervour of thy lute—
  Well may the stars be mute!

Yes, Heaven is thine; but this
  Is a world of sweets and sours;
  Our flowers are merely—flowers,
And the shadow of thy perfect bliss
  Is the sunshine of ours.

If I could dwell
Where Israfel
  Hath dwelt, and he where I,
He might not sing so wildly well
  A mortal melody,
While a bolder note than this might swell
  From my lyre within the sky.

TO HELEN

Helen, thy beauty is to me
  Like those Nicéan barks of yore,
That gently, o'er a perfumed sea,
  The weary, wayworn wanderer bore
  To his own native shore.

On desperate seas long wont to roam,
  Thy hyacinth hair, thy classic face,
Thy Naiad airs have brought me home
  To the glory that was Greece,
  And the grandeur that was Rome.

Lo! in yon brilliant window niche
  How statuelike I see thee stand,
The agate lamp within thy hand!
  Ah, Psyche, from the regions which
  Are Holy Land!

ELIZABETH

Elizabeth, it surely is most fit
(Logic and common usage so commanding)
In thy own book that *first* thy name be writ,
Zeno and other sages notwithstanding;
And *I* have other reasons for so doing
Beside my innate love of contradiction;
Each poet—*if* a poet—in pursuing
The muses thro' their bowers of Truth or Fiction,
Has studied very little of his part,
Read nothing, written less—in short's a fool
Endued with neither soul, nor sense, nor art,
Being ignorant of one important rule,
Employed in even the theses of the school—
Called—I forget the heathenish Greek name—
(Called anything, its meaning is the same)
"Always write *first* things uppermost in the heart."

ALONE

From childhood's hour I have not been
As others were—I have not seen
As others saw—I could not bring
My passions from a common spring.
From the same source I have not taken
My sorrow; I could not awaken
My heart to joy at the same tone;
And all I lov'd, *I* lov'd alone.
Then—in my childhood—in the dawn
Of a most stormy life—was drawn
From ev'ry depth of good and ill
The mystery which binds me still:
From the torrent, or the fountain,
From the red cliff of the mountain,
From the sun that 'round me roll'd
In its autumn tint of gold—
From the lightning in the sky
As it pass'd me flying by—
From the thunder and the storm,
And the cloud that took the form
(When the rest of Heaven was blue)
Of a demon in my view.

FAIRYLAND

Dim vales—and shadowy floods—
And cloudy-looking woods,
Whose forms we can't discover
For the tears that drip all over.
Huge moons there wax and wane—
Again—again—again—
Every moment of the night—
Forever changing places—
And they put out the starlight
With the breath from their pale faces.
About twelve by the moondial
One more filmy than the rest
(A kind which, upon trial,
They have found to be the best)
Comes down—still down—and down
With its center on the crown
Of a mountain's eminence,
While its wide circumference
In easy drapery falls
Over hamlets, over halls,
Wherever they may be—
O'er the strange woods—o'er the sea—
Over spirits on the wing—
Over every drowsy thing—
And buries them up quite
In a labyrinth of light—
And then, how deep!—O, deep!
Is the passion of their sleep.
In the morning they arise,
And their moony covering
Is soaring in the skies,
With the tempests as they toss,

Like—almost any thing—
Or a yellow Albatross.
They use that moon no more
For the same end as before—
Videlicet a tent—
Which I think extravagant:
Its atomies, however,
Into a shower dissever,
Of which those butterflies,
Of Earth, who seek the skies,
And so come down again
(Never-contented things!)
Have brought a specimen
Upon their quivering wings.

FAIRY LAND

Sit down beside me, Isabel,
Here, dearest, where the moonbeam fell
Just now so fairylike and well.
Now thou art dress'd for paradise!
I am star-stricken with thine eyes!
My soul is lolling on thy sighs!
Thy hair is lifted by the moon
Like flowers by the low breath of June!
Sit down, sit down—how came we here?
Or is it all but a dream, my dear?

You know that most enormous flower—
That rose—that what d' ye call it—that hung
Up like a dog-star in this bower—
Today (the wind blew, and) it swung
So impudently in my face,
So like a thing alive you know,
I tore it from its pride of place
And shook it into pieces—so
Be all ingratitude requited.
The winds ran off with it delighted,
And, thro' the opening left, as soon
As she threw off her cloak, yon moon
Has sent a ray down with a tune.
And this ray is a *fairy* ray—
Did you not say so, Isabel?
How fantastically it fell
With a spiral twist and a swell,
And over the wet grass rippled away
With a tinkling like a bell!
In my own country all the way
We can discover a moon ray

Which thro' some tatter'd curtain pries
Into the darkness of a room,
Is by (the very source of gloom)
The motes, and dust, and flies,
On which it trembles and lies
Like joy upon sorrow!
O, *when* will come the morrow?
Isabel! do you not fear
The night and the wonders here?
Dim vales! and shadowy floods!
And cloudy-looking woods
Whose forms we can't discover
For the tears that drip all over!

Huge moons—see! wax and wane
Again—again—again—
Every moment of the night—
Forever changing places!
How they put out the starlight
With the breath from their pale faces!

Lo! one is coming down
With its center on the crown
Of a mountain's eminence!
Down—still down—and down—
Now deep shall be—O deep!
The passion of our sleep!
For that wide circumference
In easy drapery falls
Drowsily over halls—
Over ruin'd walls—
Over waterfalls,
(Silent waterfalls!)
O'er the strange woods—o'er the sea—
Alas! over the sea!

TO THE RIVER

Fair river! in thy bright, clear flow
  Of crystal, wandering water,
Thou art an emblem of the glow
    Of beauty—the unhidden heart—
    The playful maziness of art
  In old Alberto's daughter;

But when within thy wave she looks—
  Which glistens then, and trembles—
Why, then, the prettiest of brooks
  Her worshipper resembles;
For in his heart, as in thy stream,
  Her image deeply lies—
His heart which trembles at the beam
  Of her soul-searching eyes.

TO——

I heed not that my earthly lot
    Hath—little of Earth in it—
That years of love have been forgot
    In the hatred of a minute:—
I mourn not that the desolate
    Are happier, sweet, than I,
But that *you* sorrow for *my* fate
    Who am a passerby.

TO——

The bowers whereat, in dreams, I see
    The wantonest singing birds,
Are lips—and all thy melody
    Of lip-begotten words—

Thine eyes, in Heaven of heart enshrined
    Then desolately fall,
O God! on my funereal mind
    Like starlight on a pall—

Thy heart—*thy* heart!—I wake and sigh,
    And sleep to dream till day
Of the truth that gold can never buy—
    Of the baubles that it may.

ROMANCE

Romance, who loves to nod and sing,
With drowsy head and folded wing,
Among the green leaves as they shake
Far down within some shadowy lake,
To me a painted paroquet
Hath been—a most familiar bird—
Taught me my alphabet to say—
To lisp my very earliest word
While in the wildwood I did lie
A child—with a most knowing eye.

Succeeding years, too wild for song,
Then roll'd like tropic storms along,
Where, tho' the garish lights that fly
Dying along the troubled sky,
Lay bare, thro' vistas thunder-riven,
The blackness of the general Heaven,
That very blackness yet doth fling
Light on the lightning's silver wing.

For, being an idle boy lang syne,
Who read Anacreon, and drank wine,
I early found Anacreon rhymes
Were almost passionate sometimes—
And by strange alchemy of brain
His pleasures always turn'd to pain—
His naivete to wild desire—
His wit to love—his wine to fire—
And so, being young and dipt in folly
I fell in love with melancholy,
And used to throw my earthly rest
And quiet all away in jest—

I could not love except where Death
Was mingling his with Beauty's breath—
Or Hymen, Time, and Destiny
Were stalking between her and me.

O, then the eternal Condor years
So shook the very Heavens on high,
With tumult as they thunder'd by;
I had no time for idle cares,
Thro' gazing on the unquiet sky!
Or if an hour with calmer wing
Its down did on my spirit fling,
That little hour with lyre and rhyme
To while away—forbidden thing!
My heart half fear'd to be a crime
Unless it trembled with the string.

But *now* my soul hath too much room—
Gone are the glory and the gloom—
The black hath mellow'd into gray,
And all the fires are fading away.

My draught of passion hath been deep—
I revell'd, and I now would sleep—
And after-drunkenness of soul
Succeeds the glories of the bowl—
An idle longing night and day
To dream my very life away.

But dreams—of those who dream as I,
Aspiringly, are damned, and die:
Yet should I swear I mean alone,
By notes so very shrilly blown,
To break upon Time's monotone,
While yet my vapid joy and grief
Are tintless of the yellow leaf—
Why not an imp the graybeard hath,
Will shake his shadow in my path—
And even the graybeard will o'erlook
Connivingly my dreaming-book.

MYSTERIOUS STAR!

Mysterious star!
Thou wert my dream
All a long summer night—
Be now my theme!
By this clear stream,
Of thee will I write;
Meantime from afar
Bathe me in light!

Thy world has not the dross of ours,
Yet all the beauty—all the flowers
That list our love, or deck our bowers
In dreamy gardens, where do lie
Dreamy maidens all the day,
While the silver winds of Circassy
On violet couches faint away.

Little—oh! little dwells in thee
Like unto what on earth we see:
Beauty's eye is here the bluest
In the falsest and untruest—
On the sweetest air doth float
The most sad and solemn note—
If with thee be broken hearts,
Joy so peacefully departs,
That its echo still doth dwell,
Like the murmur in the shell.
Thou! thy truest type of grief
Is the gently falling leaf—
Thou! thy framing is so holy
Sorrow is not melancholy.

AL AARAAF

PART I

O! Nothing earthly save the ray
(Thrown back from flowers) of Beauty's eye,
As in those gardens where the day
Springs from the gems of Circassy—
O! nothing earthly save the thrill
Of melody in woodland rill—
Or (music of the passion-hearted) .
Joy's voice so peacefully departed
That like the murmur in the shell,
Its echo dwelleth and will dwell—
Oh, nothing of the dross of ours—
Yet all the beauty—all the flowers
That list our Love, and deck our bowers—
Adorn yon world afar, afar—
The wandering star.

'T was a sweet time for Nesace—for there
Her world lay lolling on the golden air,
Near four bright suns—a temporary rest—
An oasis in desert of the blest.
Away—away—'mid seas of rays that roll
Empyrean splendor o'er th' unchained soul—
The soul that scarce (the billows are so dense)
Can struggle to its destin'd eminence—
To distant spheres, from time to time, she rode,
And late to ours, the favor'd one of God—
But, now, the ruler of an anchor'd realm,
She throws aside the scepter—leaves the helm,
And, amid incense and high spiritual hymns,
Laves in quadruple light her angel limbs.

Now happiest, loveliest in yon lovely Earth,
Whence sprang the "Idea of Beauty" into birth,
(Falling in wreaths thro' many a startled star,
Like woman's hair 'mid pearls, until, afar,
It lit on hills Achaian, and there dwelt)
She look'd into Infinity—and knelt.
Rich clouds, for canopies, about her curled—
Fit emblems of the model of her world—
Seen but in beauty—not impeding sight
Of other beauty glittering thro' the light—
A wreath that twined each starry form around,
And all the opal'd air in color bound.

   All hurriedly she knelt upon a bed
Of flowers: of lilies such as rear'd the head
On the fair Capo Deucato, and sprang
So eagerly around about to hang
Upon the flying footsteps of—deep pride—
Of her who lov'd a mortal—and so died.
The Sephalica, budding with young bees,
Uprear'd its purple stem around her knees:
And gemmy flower, of Trebizond misnam'd—
Inmate of highest stars, where erst it sham'd
All other loveliness: its honied dew
(The fabled nectar that the heathen knew)
Deliriously sweet, was dropp'd from Heaven,
And fell on gardens of the unforgiven
In Trebizond—and on a sunny flower
So like its own above that, to this hour,
It still remaineth, torturing the bee
With madness, and unwonted reverie:
In Heaven, and all its environs, the leaf
And blossom of the fairy plant, in grief
Disconsolate linger—grief that hangs her head,
Repenting follies that full long have fled,
Heaving her white breast to the balmy air,

Like guilty beauty, chasten'd, and more fair:
Nyctanthes too, as sacred as the light
She fears to perfume, perfuming the night:
And Clytia pondering between many a sun,
While pettish tears adown her petals run:
And that aspiring flower that sprang on earth—
And died, ere scarce exalted into birth,
Bursting its odorous heart in spirit to wing
Its way to Heaven, from garden of a king:
And Valisnerian lotus thither flown
From struggling with the waters of the Rhone:
And thy most lovely purple perfume, Zante!
Isola d'oro!—Fior di Levante!
And the Nelumbo bud that floats forever
With Indian Cupid down the holy river—
Fair flowers, and fairy! to whose care is given
To bear the Goddess' song, in odors, up to Heaven:

"Spirit! that dwellest where,
    In the deep sky,
The terrible and fair,
    In beauty vie!
Beyond the line of blue—
    The boundary of the star
Which turneth at the view
    Of thy barrier and thy bar—
Of the barrier overgone
    By the comets who were cast
From their pride, and from their throne
    To be drudges till the last—
To be carriers of fire
    (The red fire of their heart)
With speed that may not tire
    And with pain that shall not part—
Who livest—*that* we know—
    In Eternity—we feel—

But the shadow of whose brow
   What spirit shall reveal?
Tho' the beings whom thy Nesace,
   Thy messenger hath known
Have dream'd for thy Infinity
   A model of their own—
Thy will is done, Oh, God!
   The star hath ridden high
Thro' many a tempest, but she rode
   Beneath thy burning eye;
And here, in thought, to thee—
   In thought that can alone
Ascend thy empire and so be
   A partner of thy throne—
By winged Fantasy,
   My embassy is given,
Till secrecy shall knowledge be
   In the environs of Heaven."

She ceas'd—and buried then her burning cheek
Abash'd, amid the lilies there, to seek
A shelter from the fervor of His eye;
For the stars trembled at the Deity.
She stirr'd not—breath'd not—for a voice was there
How solemnly pervading the calm air!
A sound of silence on the startled ear
Which dreamy poets name "the music of the sphere."
Ours is a world of words: Quiet we call
"Silence"—which is the merest word of all.
All Nature speaks, and ev'n ideal things
Flap shadowy sounds from visionary wings—
But ah! not so when, thus, in realms on high
The eternal voice of God is passing by,
And the red winds are withered in the sky!

"What tho' in worlds which sightless cycles run,
Link'd to a little system, and one sun—
Where all my love is folly and the crowd
Still think my terrors but the thunder cloud,
The storm, the earthquake, and the ocean-wrath—
(Ah! will they cross me in my angrier path?)
What tho' in worlds which own a single sun
The sands of Time grow dimmer as they run,
Yet thine is my resplendency, so given
To bear my secrets thro' the upper Heaven.
Leave tenantless thy crystal home, and fly,
With all thy train, athwart the moony sky—
Apart—like fireflies in Sicilian night,
And wing to other worlds another light!
Divulge the secrets of thy embassy
To the proud orbs that twinkle—and so be
To ev'ry heart a barrier and a ban
Lest the stars totter in the guilt of man!"

Up rose the maiden in the yellow night,
The single-mooned eve!—on Earth we plight
Our faith to one love—and one moon adore—
The birthplace of young Beauty had no more.
As sprang that yellow star from downy hours
Up rose the maiden from her shrine of flowers,
And bent o'er sheeny mountain and dim plain
Her way—but left not yet her Therasæan reign.

PART II

High on a mountain of enamell'd head—
Such as the drowsy shepherd on his bed
Of giant pasturage lying at his ease,
Raising his heavy eyelid, starts and sees
With many a mutter'd "hope to be forgiven"
What time the moon is quadrated in Heaven—
Of rosy head, that towering far away
Into the sunlit ether, caught the ray
Of sunken suns at eve—at noon of night,
While the moon danc'd with the fair stranger light—
Uprear'd upon such height arose a pile
Of gorgeous columns on th' unburthen'd air,
Flashing from Parian marble that twin smile
Far down upon the wave that sparkled there,
And nursled the young mountain in its lair.
Of molten stars their pavement, such as fall
Thro' the ebon air, besilvering the pall
Of their own dissolution, while they die—
Adorning then the dwellings of the sky.
A dome, by linked light from Heaven let down,
Sat gently on these columns as a crown—
A window of one circular diamond, there,
Look'd out above into the purple air,
And rays from God shot down that meteor chain
And hallow'd all the beauty twice again,
Save when, between th' Empyrean and that ring,
Some eager spirit flapp'd his dusky wing.
But on the pillars Seraph eyes have seen
The dimness of this world; that grayish green
That Nature loves the best for Beauty's grave
Lurk'd in each cornice, round each architrave—
And every sculptur'd cherub thereabout
That from his marble dwelling peeréd out,
Seem'd earthly in the shadow of his niche—

Achaian statues in a world so rich?
Friezes from Tadmor and Persepolis—
From Balbec, and the stilly, clear abyss
Of beautiful Gomorrah! O, the wave
Is now upon thee—but too late to save!

Sound loves to revel in a summer night:
Witness the murmur of the gray twilight
That stole upon the ear, in Eyraco,
Of many a wild stargazer long ago—
That stealeth ever on the ear of him
Who, musing, gazeth on the distance dim,
And sees the darkness coming as a cloud—
Is not its form—its voice—most palpable and loud?

But what is this?—it cometh—and it brings
A music with it—'t is the rush of wings—
A pause—and then a sweeping, falling strain
And Nesace is in her halls again.
From the wild energy of wanton haste
    Her cheeks were flushing, and her lips apart;
And zone that clung around her gentle waist
    Had burst beneath the heaving of her heart.
Within the center of that hall to breathe
She paus'd and panted, Zanthe! all beneath,
The fairy light that kiss'd her golden hair
And long'd to rest, yet could but sparkle there!

Young flowers were whispering in melody
To happy flowers that night—and tree to tree;
Fountains were gushing music as they fell
In many a starlit grove, or moonlit dell;
Yet silence came upon material things—
Fair flowers, bright waterfalls and angel wings—
And sound alone that from the spirit sprang
Bore burthen to the charm the maiden sang:

" 'Neath bluebell or streamer—
   Or tufted wild spray
That keeps, from the dreamer,
   The moonbeam away—
Bright beings! that ponder,
   With half closing eyes,
On the stars which your wonder
   Hath drawn from the skies,
Till they glance thro' the shade, and
   Come down to your brow
Like—eyes of the maiden
   Who calls on you now—
Arise! from your dreaming
   In violet bowers,
To duty beseeming
   These starlitten hours—
And shake from your tresses
   Encumber'd with dew
The breath of those kisses
   That cumber them too—
(O! how, without you, Love!
   Could angels be blest?)
Those kisses of true love
   That lull'd ye to rest!
Up!—shake from your wing
   Each hindering thing:
The dew of the night—
   It would weigh down your flight;
And true love caresses—
   O! leave them apart!
They are light on the tresses,
   But lead on the heart.

"Ligeia! Ligeia!
   My beautiful one!
Whose harshest idea

Will to melody run,
O! is it thy will
　On the breezes to toss?
Or, capriciously still,
　Like the lone Albatross,
Incumbent on night
　(As she on the air)
To keep watch with delight
　On the harmony there?

"Ligeia! wherever
　Thy image may be,
No magic shall sever
　Thy music from thee.
Thou hast bound many eyes
　In a dreamy sleep—
But the strains still arise
　Which *thy* vigilance keep—
The sound of the rain
　Which leaps down to the flower,
And dances again
　In the rhythm of the shower—
The murmur that springs
　From the growing of grass
Are the music of things—
　But are modell'd, alas!—
Away, then my dearest,
　O! hie thee away
To springs that lie clearest
　Beneath the moon-ray—
To lone lake that smiles,
　In its dream of deep rest,
At the many star-isles
　That enjewel its breast—
Where wild flowers, creeping,
　Have mingled their shade,

On its margin is sleeping
    Full many a maid—
Some have left the cool glade, and
    Have slept with the bee—
Arouse them my maiden,
    On moorland and lea—
Go! breathe on their slumber,
    All softly in ear,
The musical number
    They slumber'd to hear—
For what can awaken
    An angel so soon
Whose sleep hath been taken
    Beneath the cold moon,
As the spell which no slumber
    Of witchery may test,
The rhythmical number
    Which lull'd him to rest?"

Spirits in wing, and angels to the view,
A thousand seraphs burst th' Empyrean thro',
Young dreams still hovering on their drowsy flight—
Seraphs in all but "Knowledge," the keen light
That fell, refracted, thro' thy bounds afar,
O Death! from eye of God upon that star:
Sweet was that error—sweeter still that death—
Sweet was that error—ev'n with *us* the breath
Of Science dims the mirror of our joy—
To them 't were the Simoom, and would destroy—
For what (to them) availeth it to know
That Truth is Falsehood—or that Bliss is Woe?
Sweet was their death—with them to die was rife
With the last ecstasy of satiate life—
Beyond that death no immortality—
But sleep that pondereth and is not "to be"—

And there—oh! may my weary spirit dwell—
Apart from Heaven's Eternity—and yet how far from Hell!

What guilty spirit, in what shrubbery dim,
Heard not the stirring summons of that hymn?
But two: they fell: for Heaven no grace imparts
To those who hear not for their beating hearts.
A maiden-angel and her seraph-lover—
O! where (and ye may seek the wide skies over)
Was Love, the blind, near sober Duty known?
Unguided Love hath fallen—'mid "tears of perfect moan."

He was a goodly spirit—he who fell:
A wanderer by moss-y-mantled well—
A gazer on the lights that shine above—
A dreamer in the moonbeam by his love:
What wonder? for each star is eye-like there,
And looks so sweetly down on Beauty's hair—
And they, and ev'ry mossy spring were holy
To his love-haunted heart and melancholy.
The night had found (to him a night of wo)
Upon a mountain crag, young Angelo—
Beetling it bends athwart the solemn sky,
And scowls on starry worlds that down beneath it lie.
Here sate he with his love—his dark eye bent
With eagle gaze along the firmament:
Now turn'd it upon her—but ever then
It trembled to the orb of EARTH again.

"Ianthe, dearest, see! how dim that ray!
How lovely 't is to look so far away!
She seem'd not thus upon that autumn eve
I left her gorgeous halls—nor mourn'd to leave.
That eve—that eve—I should remember well—
The sunray dropp'd, in Lemnos, with a spell

On th' Arabesque carving of a gilded hall
Wherein I sate, and on the draperied wall—
And on my eyelids—O the heavy light!
How drowsily it weigh'd them into night!
On flowers, before, and mist, and love they ran
With Persian Saadi in his Gulistan:
But O that light!—I slumber'd—Death, the while,
Stole o'er my senses in that lovely isle
So softly that no single silken hair
Awoke that slept—or knew that he was there.

The last spot of Earth's orb I trod upon
Was a proud temple call'd the Parthenon—
More beauty clung around her column'd wall
Than ev'n thy glowing bosom beats withal,
And when old Time my wing did disenthral
Thence sprang I—as the eagle from his tower,
And years I left behind me in an hour.
What time upon her airy bounds I hung
One half the garden of her globe was flung
Unrolling as a chart unto my view—
Tenantless cities of the desert too!
Ianthe, beauty crowded on me then,
And half I wish'd to be again of men."

"My Angelo! and why of them to be?
A brighter dwelling place is there for thee—
And greener fields than in yon world above,
And woman's loveliness—and passionate love."

"But, list, Ianthe! when the air so soft
Fail'd, as my pennon'd spirit leapt aloft,
Perhaps my brain grew dizzy—but the world
I left so late was into chaos hurl'd—
Sprang from her station, on the winds apart,

And roll'd, a flame, the fiery Heaven athwart.
Methought, my sweet one, then I ceased to soar
And fell—not swiftly as I rose before,
But with a downward, tremulous motion thro'
Light, brazen rays, this golden star unto!
Nor long the measure of my falling hours,
For nearest of all stars was thine to ours—
Dread star! that came, amid a night of mirth,
A red Dædalion on the timid Earth.

"We came—and to thy Earth—but not to us
Be given our lady's bidding to discuss:
We came, my love; around, above, below,
Gay firefly of the night we come and go,
Nor ask a reason save the angel-nod
She grants to us, as granted by her God—
But, Angelo, than thine gray Time unfurl'd
Never his fairy wing o'er fairer world!
Dim was its little disk, and angel eyes
Alone could see the phantom in the skies,
When first Al Aaraaf knew her course to be
Headlong thitherward o'er the starry sea—
But when its glory swell'd upon the sky,
As glowing Beauty's bust beneath man's eye,
We paus'd before the heritage of men,
And thy star trembled—as doth Beauty then!"

Thus, in discourse, the lovers whiled away
The night that waned and waned and brought no day.
They fell: for Heaven to them no hope imparts
Who hear not for the beating of their hearts.

SONNET—TO SCIENCE

Science! true daughter of Old Time thou art!
  Who alterest all things with thy peering eyes.
Why preyest thou thus upon the poet's heart,
  Vulture, whose wings are dull realities?
How should he love thee? or how deem thee wise,
  Who wouldst not leave him in his wandering
To seek for treasure in the jewelled skies,
  Albeit he soared with an undaunted wing?
Hast thou not dragged Diana from her car?
  And driven the Hamadryad from the wood
To seek a shelter in some happier star?
  Hast thou not torn the Naiad from her flood,
The Elfin from the green grass, and from me
The summer dream beneath the tamarind tree?

THE LAKE: TO—

In spring of youth it was my lot
To haunt of the wide world a spot
The which I could not love the less—
So lovely was the loneliness
Of a wild lake, with black rock bound,
And the tall pines that towered around.

But when the Night had thrown her pall
Upon that spot, as upon all,
And the mystic wind went by
Murmuring in melody—
Then—ah then I would awake
To the terror of the lone lake.

Yet the terror was not fright,
But a tremulous delight—
A feeling not the jewelled mine
Could teach or bribe me to define—
Nor Love—although the Love were thine.

Death was in that poisonous wave,
And in its gulf a fitting grave
For him who thence could solace bring
To his lone imagining—
Whose solitary soul could make
An Eden of that dim lake.

"THE HAPPIEST DAY—THE HAPPIEST HOUR"

The happiest day—the happiest hour
  My sear'd and blighted heart hath known,
The highest hope of pride, and power,
  I feel hath flown.

Of power! said I? yes! such I ween
  But they have vanish'd long alas!
The visions of my youth have been—
  But let them pass.

And, pride, what have I now with thee?
  Another brow may ev'n inherit
The venom thou hast pour'd on me—
  Be still my spirit.

The happiest day—the happiest hour
  Mine eyes shall see—have ever seen
The brightest glance of pride and power
  I feel—have been:

But were that hope of pride and power
  Now offer'd, with the pain
Ev'n *then* I felt—that brightest hour
  I would not live again:

For on its wing was dark alloy
  And as it flutter'd—fell
An essence—powerful to destroy
  A soul that knew it well.

A DREAM

In visions of the dark night
　　I have dreamed of joy departed—
But a waking dream of life and light
　　Hath left me brokenhearted.

Ah! what is not a dream by day
　　To him whose eyes are cast
On things around him with a ray
　　Turned back upon the past?

That holy dream—that holy dream,
　　While all the world were chiding,
Hath cheered me as a lovely beam
　　A lonely spirit guiding.

What though that light, thro' storm and night,
　　So trembled from afar—
What could there be more purely bright
　　In Truth's daystar?

STANZAS

How often we forget all time, when lone
Admiring Nature's universal throne;
Her woods—her wilds—her mountains—the intense
Reply of hers to our intelligence!

[—BYRON: *The Island.*]

1

In youth have I known one with whom the Earth
In secret communing held—as he with it,
In daylight, and in beauty from his birth:
Whose fervid, flick'ring torch of life was lit
From the sun and stars, whence he had drawn forth
A passionate light—such for his spirit was fit—
And yet that spirit knew—not in the hour
Of its own fervor—what had o'er it power.

2

Perhaps it may be that my mind is wrought
To a fever by the moon beam that hangs o'er,
But I will half believe that wild light fraught
With more of sov'reignty than ancient lore
Hath ever told—or is it of a thought
The unembodied essence, and no more
That with a quick'ning spell doth o'er us pass
As dew of the nighttime, o'er the summer grass?

3

Doth o'er us pass, when, as th' expanding eye
To the lov'd object—so the tear to the lid
Will start, which lately slept in apathy?
And yet it need not be—(that object) hid
From us in life—but common—which doth lie
Each hour before us—but *then* only bid
With a strange sound, as of a harp string broken
T' awake us—'Tis a symbol and a token.

4

Of what in other worlds shall be—and giv'n
In beauty by our God, to those alone
Who otherwise would fall from life and Heav'n
Drawn by their heart's passion, and that tone,
That high tone of the spirit which hath striv'n
Tho' not with Faith—with godliness—whose throne
With desp'rate energy 't hath beaten down;
Wearing its own deep feeling as a crown.

IMITATION

A dark unfathom'd tide
Of interminable pride—
A mystery, and a dream,
Should my early life seem;
I say that dream was fraught
With a wild, and waking thought
Of beings that have been,
Which my spirit hath not seen,
Had I let them pass me by,
With a dreaming eye!
Let none of earth inherit
That vision on my spirit;
Those thoughts I would control,
As a spell upon his soul:
For that bright hope at last
And that light time have past,
And my worldly rest hath gone
With a sight as it pass'd on:
I care not tho' it perish
With a thought I then did cherish.

EVENING STAR

'Twas noontide of summer.
  And mid-time of night:
And stars, in their orbits.
  Shone pale, thro' the light
Of the brighter, cold moon,
  'Mid planets her slaves,
Herself in the Heavens,
  Her beam on the waves.
  I gaz'd awhile
  On her cold smile;
Too cold—too cold for me—
  There pass'd, as a shroud,
  A fleecy cloud,
And I turn'd away to thee,
  Proud Evening Star,
  In thy glory afar,
And dearer thy beam shall be;
  For joy to my heart
  Is the proud part
Thou bearest in Heav'n at night,
  And more I admire
  Thy distant fire,
Than that colder, lowly light.

SPIRITS OF THE DEAD

I

Thy soul shall find itself alone
'Mid dark thoughts of the gray tombstone—
Not one, of all the crowd, to pry
Into thine hour of secrecy:

II

Be silent in that solitude,
    Which is not loneliness—for then
The spirits of the dead who stood
    In life before thee are again
In death around thee—and their will
Shall overshadow thee: be still.

III

The night—tho' clear—shall frown—
And the stars shall look not down.
From their high thrones in the heaven,
With light like Hope to mortals given—
But their red orbs, without beam,
To thy weariness shall seem
As a burning and a fever
Which would cling to thee forever.

IV

Now are thoughts thou shalt not banish—
Now are visions ne'er to vanish—
From thy spirit shall they pass
No more—like dewdrop from the grass.

V

The breeze—the breath of God—is still—
And the mist upon the hill
Shadowy—shadowy—yet unbroken,
Is a symbol and a token—
How it hangs upon the trees,
A mystery of mysteries!—

DREAMS

Oh! that my young life were a lasting dream!
My spirit not awakening, till the beam
Of an Eternity should bring the morrow.
Yes! tho' that long dream were of hopeless sorrow,
'T were better than the cold reality
Of waking life to him whose heart must be,
And hath been still, upon the lovely earth,
A chaos of deep passion, from his birth.

But should it be—that dream eternally
Continuing—as dreams have been to me
In my young boyhood—should it thus be given,
'T were folly still to hope for higher Heaven.
For I have revell'd when the sun was bright
I' the summer sky, in dreams of living light,
And loveliness,—have left my very heart
In climes of mine imagining, apart
From mine own home, with beings that have been
Of mine own thought—what more could I have seen?

'T was once—and *only* once—and the wild hour
From my remembrance shall not pass—some power
Or spell had bound me—'t was the chilly wind
Came o'er me in the night, and left behind
Its image on my spirit—or the moon
Shone on my slumbers in her lofty noon
Too coldly—or the stars—howe'er it was
That dream was as that night wind—let it pass.

I *have been* happy, tho' [but] in a dream.
I have been happy—and I love the theme:
Dreams! in their vivid coloring of life
As in that fleeting, shadowy, misty strife
Of semblance with reality which brings
To the delirious eye more lovely things
Of Paradise and Love—and all our own!
Than young Hope in his sunniest hour hath known.

SONG

I saw thee on thy bridal day—
   When a burning blush came o'er thee,
Though happiness around thee lay,
   The world all love before thee:

And in thine eye a kindling light
   (Whatever it might be)
Was all on Earth my aching sight
   Of Loveliness could see.

That blush, perhaps, was maiden shame—
   As such it well may pass—
Though its glow hath raised a fiercer flame
   In the breast of him, alas!

Who saw thee on that bridal day,
   When that deep blush *would* come o'er thee,
Though happiness around thee lay,
   The world all love before thee.

TAMERLANE

Kind solace in a dying hour!
  Such, father, is not (now) my theme—
I will not madly deem that power
    Of Earth may shrive me of the sin
    Unearthly pride hath revell'd in—
I have no time to dote or dream:
You call it hope—that fire of fire!
It is but agony of desire:
If I *can* hope—Oh God! I can—
  Its fount is holier—more divine—
I would not call thee fool, old man,
    But such is not a gift of thine.

Know thou the secret of a spirit
  Bow'd from its wild pride into shame.
O yearning heart! I did inherit
  Thy withering portion with the fame,
The searing glory which hath shone
Amid the Jewels of my throne,
Halo of Hell! and with a pain
Not Hell shall make me fear again—
O craving heart, for the lost flowers
And sunshine of my summer hours!
The undying voice of that dead time,
With its interminable chime,
Rings, in the spirit of a spell,
Upon thy emptiness—a knell.

I have not always been as now:
The fever'd diadem on my brow
  I claim'd and won usurpingly——
Hath not the same fierce heirdom given

Rome to the Cæsar—this to me?
  The heritage of a kingly mind,
And a proud spirit which hath striven
  Triumphantly with human kind.

On mountain soil I first drew life:
  The mists of the Taglay have shed
  Nightly their dews upon my head,
And, I believe, the winged strife
And tumult of the headlong air
Have nestled in my very hair.

So late from Heaven—that dew—it fell
  ('Mid dreams of an unholy night)
Upon me with the touch of Hell,
  While the red flashing of the light
From clouds that hung, like banners, o'er,
  Appeared to my half-closing eye
  The pageantry of monarchy,
And the deep trumpet-thunder's roar
  Came hurriedly upon me, telling
    Of human battle, where my voice,
    My own voice, silly child!—was swelling
      (O! how my spirit would rejoice,
And leap within me at the cry)
The battlecry of Victory!

The rain came down upon my head
  Unshelter'd—and the heavy wind
  Rendered me mad and deaf and blind.
It was but man, I thought, who shed
  Laurels upon me: and the rush—
The torrent of the chilly air
Gurgled within my ear the crush
  Of empires—with the captive's prayer—
The hum of suitors—and the tone
Of flattery 'round a sovereign's throne.

My passions, from that hapless hour,
　　Usurp'd a tyranny which men
Have deem'd, since I have reach'd to power,
　　My innate nature—be it so:
　　But, father, there liv'd one who, then,
Then—in my boyhood—when their fire
　　Burn'd with a still intenser glow
(For passion must, with youth, expire)
　　E'en *then* who knew this iron heart
　　In woman's weakness had a part.

I have no words—alas!—to tell
The loveliness of loving well!
Nor would I now attempt to trace
The more than beauty of a face
Whose lineaments, upon my mind,
Are——shadows on th' unstable wind:
Thus I remember having dwelt
　　Some page of early lore upon,
With loitering eye, till I have felt
The letters—with their meaning—melt
　　To fantasies—with none.

O, she was worthy of all love!
　　Love—as in infancy was mine—
'Twas such as angel minds above
　　Might envy; her young heart the shrine
On which my every hope and thought
　　Were incense—then a goodly gift,
　　For they were childish and upright—
Pure——as her young example taught:
　　Why did I leave it, and, adrift,
　　Trust to the fire within, for light?

We grew in age—and love—together—
　　Roaming the forest, and the wild;
My breast her shield in wintry weather—

And, when the friendly sunshine smil'd,
And she would mark the opening skies,
I saw no Heaven—but in her eyes.

Young Love's first lesson is——the heart:
   For 'mid that sunshine, and those smiles,
When, from our little cares apart,
   And laughing at her girlish wiles,
I'd throw me on her throbbing breast,
   And pour my spirit out in tears—
There was no need to speak the rest—
   No need to quiet any fears
Of her—who ask'd no reason why,
But turn'd on me her quiet eye!

Yet *more* than worthy of the love
My spirit struggled with, and strove,
When, on the mountain peak, alone,
Ambition lent it a new tone—
I had no being—but in thee:
   The world, and all it did contain
In the earth—the air—the sea—
   Its joy—its little lot of pain
That was new pleasure——the ideal,
   Dim, vanities of dreams by night—
And dimmer nothings which were real—
   (Shadows—and a more shadowy light!)
Parted upon their misty wings,
     And, so, confusedly, became
     Thine image and—a name—a name!
Two separate—yet most intimate things.

I was ambitious—have you known
     The passion, father? You have not:
A cottager, I mark'd a throne
Of half the world as all my own,
     And murmur'd at such lowly lot—

But, just like any other dream,
        Upon the vapor of the dew
My own had past, did not the beam
        Of beauty which did while it thro'
The minute—the hour—the day—oppress
My mind with double loveliness.

We walk'd together on the crown
Of a high mountain which look'd down
Afar from its proud natural towers
        Of rock and forest, on the hills—
The dwindled hills! begirt with bowers
        And shouting with a thousand rills.

I spoke to her of power and pride,
        But mystically—in such guise
That she might deem it nought beside
        The moment's converse; in her eyes
I read, perhaps too carelessly—
        A mingled feeling with my own—
The flush on her bright cheek, to me
        Seem'd to become a queenly throne
Too well that I should let it be
        Light in the wilderness alone.

I wrapp'd myself in grandeur then
        And donn'd a visionary crown——
                Yet it was not that Fantasy
                Had thrown her mantle over me—
But that, among the rabble—men,
        Lion ambition is chain'd down—
And crouches to a keeper's hand—
Not so in deserts where the grand—
The wild—the terrible conspire
With their own breath to fan his fire.

Look 'round thee now on Samarcand!—
   Is she not queen of Earth? her pride
Above all cities? in her hand
   Their destinies? in all beside
Of glory which the world hath known
Stands she not nobly and alone?
Falling—her veriest steppingstone
Shall form the pedestal of a throne—
And who her sovereign? Timour—he
   Whom the astonished people saw
Striding o'er empires haughtily
   A diadem'd outlaw!

O, human love! thou spirit given,
On Earth, of all we hope in Heaven!
Which fall'st into the soul like rain
Upon the Siroc-wither'd plain,
And, failing in thy power to bless,
But leav'st the heart a wilderness!
Idea! which bindest life around
With music of so strange a sound
And beauty of so wild a birth—
Farewell! for I have won the Earth.

When Hope, the eagle that tower'd, could see
   No cliff beyond him in the sky,
His pinions were bent droopingly—
   And homeward turn'd his soften'd eye.
'T was sunset: when the sun will part
There comes a sullenness of heart
To him who still would look upon
The glory of the summer sun.
That soul will hate the ev'ning mist
So often lovely, and will list
To the sound of the coming darkness (known
To those whose spirits harken) as one

Who, in a dream of night, *would* fly
But *cannot* from a danger nigh.

What tho' the moon—the white moon
Shed all the splendor of her noon,
Her smile is chilly—and *her* beam,
In that time of dreariness, will seem
(So like you gather in your breath)
A portrait taken after death.
And boyhood is a summer sun
Whose waning is the dreariest one—
For all we live to know is known
And all we seek to keep hath flown—
Let life, then, as the dayflower, fall
With the noonday beauty—which is all.

I reach'd my home—my home no more—
   For all had flown who made it so.
I pass'd from out its mossy door,
   And, tho' my tread was soft and low,
A voice came from the threshold stone
Of one whom I had earlier known—
   O, I defy thee, Hell, to show
   On beds of fire that burn below,
   An humbler heart—a deeper woe.

Father, I firmly do believe—
   I *know*—for Death who comes for me
    From regions of the blest afar,
Where there is nothing to deceive,
    Hath left his iron gate ajar,
   And rays of truth you cannot see
   Are flashing thro' Eternity——
I do believe that Eblis hath
A snare in every human path—

Else how, when in the holy grove
I wandered of the idol, Love,
Who daily scents his snowy wings
With incense of burnt offerings
From the most unpolluted things,
Whose pleasant bowers are yet so riven
Above with trellic'd rays from Heaven
No mote may shun—no tiniest fly—
The light'ning of his eagle eye—
How was it that Ambition crept,
   Unseen, amid the revels there,
Till growing bold, he laughed and leapt
   In the tangles of Love's very hair?

O, TEMPORA! O, MORES!

O, Times! O, Manners! It is my opinion
That you are changing sadly your dominion—
I mean the reign of manners hath long ceased,
For men have none at all, or bad at least;
And as for times, altho' 'tis said by many
The "good old times" were far the worst of any,
Of which sound doctrine I believe each tittle,
Yet still I think these worse than them a little.

I've been a thinking—isn't that the phrase?—
I like your Yankee words and Yankee ways—
I've been a thinking, whether it were best
To take things seriously, or all in jest;
Whether, with grim Heraclitus of yore,
To weep, as he did, till his eyes were sore;
Or rather laugh with him, that queer philosopher,
Democritus of Thrace, who used to toss over
The page of life and grin at the dog-ears,
As though he'd say, "Why, who the devil cares?"

This is a question which, oh heaven, withdraw
The luckless query from a member's claw!
Instead of two sides, Job has nearly eight,
Each fit to furnish forth four hours debate.
What shall be done? I'll lay it on the table,
And take the matter up when I'm more able;
And, in the meantime, to prevent all bother,
I'll neither laugh with one, nor cry with t'other,
Nor deal in flatt'ry or aspersions foul,
But, taking one by each hand, merely growl.

Ah, growl, say you, my friend, and pray at what?
Why, really, sir, I almost had forgot—
But, damn it, sir, I deem it a disgrace
That things should stare us boldly in the face,
And daily strut the street with bows and scrapes,
Who would be men by imitating apes.
I beg your pardon, reader, for the oath
The monkeys make me swear, though something loth;
I'm apt to be discursive in my style,
But pray be patient; yet a little while
Will change me, and as politicians do,
I'll mend my manners and my measures too.

Of all the cities—and I've seen no few;
For I have travelled, friend, as well as you—
I don't remember one, upon my soul,
But take it generally upon the whole,
(As members say they like their logic taken,
Because divided, it may chance be shaken)
So pat, agreeable and vastly proper
As this for a neat, frisky counter-hopper;
Here he may revel to his heart's content,
Flounce like a fish in his own element,
Toss back his fine curls from their forehead fair,
And hop o'er counters with a Vester's air,
Complete at night what he began A.M.,
And having cheated ladies, dance with them;
For, at a ball, what fair one can escape
The pretty little hand that sold her tape,
Or who so cold, so callous to refuse
The youth who cut the ribbon for her shoes!

One of these fish, *par excellence* the beau—
God help me!—it has been my lot to know,
At least by sight, for I'm a timid man,
And always keep from laughing, if I can;

But speak to him, he'll make you such grimace,
Lord! to be grave exceeds the power of face.
The hearts of all the ladies are with him,
Their bright eyes on his Tom and Jerry brim
And dovetailed coat, obtained at cost; while then
Those eyes won't turn on anything like men.

His very voice is musical delight,
His form, once seen, becomes a part of sight;
In short, his shirt collar, his look, his tone is
The "beau ideal" fancied for Adonis.
Philosophers have often held dispute
As to the seat of thought in man and brute;
For that the power of thought attends the latter
My friend, the beau, hath made a settled matter,
And spite of all dogmas, current in all ages,
One settled fact is better than ten sages.

For he does think, though I am oft in doubt
If I can tell exactly what about.
Ah, yes! his little foot and ankle trim,
'Tis there the seat of reason lies in him,
A wise philosopher would shake his head,
He then, of course, must shake his foot instead.
At me, in vengeance, shall that foot be shaken—
Another proof of thought, I'm not mistaken—
Because to his cat's eyes I hold a glass,
And let him see himself, a proper ass!
I think he'll take this likeness to himself,
But if he won't, *he shall*, a stupid elf,
And, lest the guessing throw the fool in fits,
I close the portrait with the name of Pitts.

SCENES FROM "POLITIAN"

AN UNPUBLISHED DRAMA

I

ROME —*A Hall in a Palace. Alessandra and Castiglione.*

ALESSANDRA. Thou art sad, Castiglione.

CASTIGLIONE. Sad!—not I.
Oh, I'm the happiest, happiest man in Rome!
A few days more, thou knowest, my Alessandra,
Will make thee mine. Oh, I am very happy!

ALESS. Methinks thou hast a singular way of showing
Thy happiness!—what ails thee, cousin of mine?
Why didst thou sigh so deeply?

CAS. Did I sigh?
I was not conscious of it. It is a fashion,
A silly—a most silly fashion I have
When I am *very* happy. Did I sigh? (*sighing.*)

ALESS. Thou didst. Thou art not well. Thou hast indulged
Too much of late, and I am vexed to see it.
Late hours and wine, Castiglione,—these
Will ruin thee! thou art already altered—
Thy looks are haggard—nothing so wears away
The constitution as late hours and wine.

CAS. (*musing.*) Nothing, fair cousin, nothing—not even
      deep sorrow—
Wears it away like evil hours and wine.
I will amend.

ALESS. Do it! I would have thee drop
Thy riotous company, too—fellows low born—
Ill suit the like with old Di Broglio's heir
And Alessandra's husband.

CAS. I will drop them.

ALESS. Thou wilt—thou must. Attend thou also more

To thy dress and equipage—they are over plain
For thy lofty rank and fashion—much depends
Upon appearances.

    CAS. I'll see to it.

    ALESS. Then see to it!—pay more attention, sir,
To a becoming carriage—much thou wantest
In dignity.

    CAS. Much, much, oh much I want
In proper dignity.

    ALESS. (*haughtily.*) Thou mockest me, sir!

    CAS. (*abstractedly.*) Sweet, gentle Lalage!

    ALESS. Heard I aright?
I speak to him—he speaks of Lalage!
Sir Count! (*places her hand on his shoulder*) what art thou
    dreaming? he's not well!
What ails thee, sir?

    CAS. (*starting.*) Cousin! fair cousin!—madam!
I crave thy pardon—indeed I am not well—
Your hand from off my shoulder, if you please.
This air is most oppressive!—Madam—the Duke!

            Enter Di Broglio.

    DI BROGLIO. My son, I've news for thee!—hey?—
    what's the matter? (*observing Alessandra.*)
I' the pouts? Kiss her, Castiglione! kiss her,
You dog! and make it up, I say, this minute!
I've news for you both. Politian is expected
Hourly in Rome—Politian, Earl of Leicester!
We'll have him at the wedding. 'Tis his first visit
To the imperial city.

    ALESS. What! Politian
Of Britain, Earl of Leicester?

    DI BROG. The same, my love.
We'll have him at the wedding. A man quite young
In years, but gray in fame. I have not seen him,
But Rumor speaks of him as of a prodigy
Preeminent in arts and arms, and wealth,

And high descent. We'll have him at the wedding.

ALESS. I have heard much of this Politian.
Gay, volatile and giddy—is he not?
And little given to thinking.

DI BROG. Far from it, love.
No branch, they say, of all philosophy
So deep abstruse he has not mastered it.
Learned as few are learned.

ALESS. 'Tis very strange!
I have known men have seen Politian
And sought his company. They speak of him
As of one who entered madly into life.
Drinking the cup of pleasure to the dregs.

CAS. Ridiculous! Now *I* have seen Politian
And know him well—nor learned nor mirthful he.
He is a dreamer and a man shut out
From common passions.

DI BROG. Children, we disagree.
Let us go forth and taste the fragrant air
Of the garden. Did I dream, or did I hear
Politian was a *melancholy* man? (*exeunt.*)

II

ROME. *A Lady's apartment, with a window open and looking into a garden. Lalage, in deep mourning, reading at a table on which lie some books and a hand mirror. In the background Jacinta (a servant maid) leans carelessly upon a chair.*

LAL. Jacinta! is it thou?

JAC. (*pertly.*) Yes, Ma'am, I'm here.

LAL. I did not know, Jacinta, you were in waiting.
Sit down!—let not my presence trouble you—
Sit down!—for I am humble, most humble.

JAC. (*aside.*) 'Tis time.

(Jacinta seats herself in a sidelong manner upon the chair, resting her elbows upon the back, and regarding her mistress with a contemptuous look. Lalage continues to read.)

LAL. "It in another climate, so he said,
Bore a bright golden flower, but not i' this soil!"
(pauses—turns over some leaves, and resumes.)
"No lingering winters there, nor snow, nor shower—
But Ocean ever to refresh mankind
Breathes the shrill spirit of the western wind."
Oh, beautiful!—most beautiful!—how like
To what my fevered soul doth dream of Heaven!
O happy land! *(pauses.)* She died!—the maiden died!
O still more happy maiden who couldst die!
Jacinta!
(Jacinta returns no answer, and Lalage presently resumes.)
Again!—a similar tale
Told of a beauteous dame beyond the sea!
Thus speaketh one Ferdinand in the words of the play—
"She died full young"—one Bossola answers him—
"I think not so—her infelicity
Seemed to have years too many"—Ah luckless lady!
Jacinta! *(still no answer.)*
     Here's a far sterner story
But like—oh, very like in its despair—.
Of that Egyptian queen, winning so easily
A thousand hearts—losing at length her own.
She died. Thus endeth the history—and her maids
Lean over her and weep—two gentle maids
With gentle names—Eiros and Charmion!
Rainbow and Dove!——Jacinta!
     JAC. *(pettishly.)* Madam, what *is* it?
     LAL. Wilt thou, my good Jacinta, be so kind
As go down in the library and bring me
The Holy Evangelists.
     JAC. Pshaw! *(exit.)*

LAL. If there be balm
For the wounded spirit in Gilead it is there!
Dew in the night time of my bitter trouble
Will there be found—"dew sweeter far than that
Which hangs like chains of pearl on Hermon hill."
  (*re-enter Jacinta, and throws a volume on the table.*)
  JAC. There, ma'am, 's the book. Indeed she is very trouble
  some. (*aside.*)
  LAL. (*astonished.*) What didst thou say, Jacinta? Have I
  done aught
To grieve thee or to vex thee?—I am sorry.
For thou hast served me long and ever been
Trustworthy and respectful. (*resumes her reading.*)
  JAC. I can't believe
She has any more jewels—no—no—she gave me all.
  (*aside.*)
  LAL. What didst thou say, Jacinta? Now I bethink me
Thou hast not spoken lately of thy wedding.
How fares good Ugo?—and when is it to be?
Can I do aught?—is there no farther aid
Thou needest, Jacinta?
  JAC. Is there no *farther* aid!
That's meant for me. (*aside*) I'm sure, Madam, you need not
Be always throwing those jewels in my teeth.
  LAL. Jewels! Jacinta,—now indeed, Jacinta,
I thought not of the jewels.
  JAC. Oh! perhaps not!
But then I might have sworn it. After all,
There's Ugo says the ring is only paste,
For he's sure the Count Castiglione never
Would have given a real diamond to such as you;
And at the best I'm certain, Madam, you cannot
Have use for jewels *now*. But I might have sworn it. (*exit.*)
  (*Lalage bursts into tears and leans her head upon the
    table—after a short pause raises it.*)
  LAL. Poor Lalage!—and is it come to this?

Thy servant maid!—but courage!—'tis but a viper
Whom thou hast cherished to sting thee to the soul!
                    (*taking up the mirror.*)
Ha! here at least's a friend—too much a friend
In earlier days—a friend will not deceive thee.
Fair mirror and true! now tell me (for thou canst)
A tale—a pretty tale—and heed thou not
Though it be rife with woe. It answers me.
It speaks of sunken eyes, and wasted cheeks,
And Beauty long deceased—remembers me
Of Joy departed—Hope, the Seraph Hope,
Inurned and entombed!—now, in a tone
Low, sad, and solemn, but most audible,
Whispers of early grave untimely yawning
For ruined maid. Fair mirror and true!—thou liest not!
Thou hast no end to gain—no heart to break—
Castiglione lied who said he loved——
Thou true—he false!—false!—false!
          (*while she speaks, a monk enters her apartment,
                and approaches unobserved.*)
     MONK. Refuge thou hast,
Sweet daughter! in Heaven. Think of eternal things!
Give up thy soul to penitence, and pray!
     LAL. (*arising hurriedly.*) I *cannot* pray!—My soul is at
        war with God!
The frightful sounds of merriment below
Disturb my senses—go! I cannot pray—
The sweet airs from the garden worry me!
Thy presence grieves me—go!—thy priestly raiment
Fills me with dread—thy ebony crucifix
With horror and awe!
     MONK. Think of thy precious soul!
     LAL. Think of my early days!—think of my father
And mother in Heaven! think of our quiet home,
And the rivulet that ran before the door!
Think of my little sisters!—think of them!

And think of me!—think of my trusting love
And confidence—his vows—my ruin—think—think
Of my unspeakable misery!——begone!
Yet stay! yet stay!—what was it thou saidst of prayer
And penitence? Didst thou not speak of faith
And vows before the throne?

    MONK. I did.

    LAL. 'Tis well.

There *is* a vow were fitting should be made—
A sacred vow, imperative, and urgent,
A solemn vow!

    MONK. Daughter, this zeal is well!

    LAL. Father, this zeal is anything but well!

Hast thou a crucifix fit for this thing?
A crucifix whereon to register
This sacred vow? (*he hands her his own.*)
Not that—Oh! no!—no!—no! (*shuddering.*)
Not that! Not that!—I tell thee, holy man,
Thy raiments and thy ebony cross affright me!
Stand back! I have a crucifix myself,—
I have a crucifix! Methinks 'twere fitting
The deed—the vow—the symbol of the deed—
And the deed's register should tally, father!

    (*draws a cross-handled dagger and raises it on high.*)
Behold the cross wherewith a vow like mine
Is written in Heaven!

    MONK. Thy words are madness, daughter,

And speak a purpose unholy—thy lips are livid—
Thine eyes are wild—tempt not the wrath divine!
Pause ere too late!—oh be not—be not rash!
Swear not the oath—oh swear it not!

    LAL. 'Tis sworn!

III

An apartment in a palace. Politian and Baldazzar.

BALDAZZAR. ——Arouse thee now, Politian!
Thou must not—nay indeed, indeed, thou shalt not
Give way unto these humors. Be thyself!
Shake off the idle fancies that beset thee,
And live, for now thou diest!
POLITIAN. Not so, Baldazzar!
Surely I live.
BAL. Politian, it doth grieve me
To see thee thus.
POL. Baldazzar, it doth grieve me
To give thee cause for grief, my honored friend.
Command me, sir! what wouldst thou have me do?
At thy behest I will shake off that nature
Which from my forefathers I did inherit,
Which with my mother's milk I did imbibe,
And be no more Politian, but some other.
Command me, sir!
BAL. To the field then—to the field—
To the senate or the field.
POL. Alas! alas!
There is an imp would follow me even there!
There is an imp *hath* followed me even there!
There is——what voice was that?
BAL. I heard it not.
I heard not any voice except thine own,
And the echo of thine own.
POL. Then I but dreamed.
BAL. Give not thy soul to dreams: the camp—the court
Befit thee—Fame awaits thee—Glory calls—
And her the trumpet-tongued thou wilt not hear
In hearkening to imaginary sounds
And phantom voices.

POL. It *is* a phantom voice!
Didst thou not hear it *then?*

BAL. I heard it not.

POL. Thou heardst it not!——Baldazzar, speak no more
To me, Politian, of thy camps and courts.
Oh! I am sick, sick, sick, even unto death,
Of the hollow and high-sounding vanities
Of the populous Earth! Bear with me yet awhile!
We have been boys together—schoolfellows—
And now are friends—yet shall not be so long—
For in the eternal city thou shalt do me
A kind and gentle office, and a Power—
A Power august, benignant and supreme—
Shall then absolve thee of all farther duties
Unto thy friend.

BAL. Thou speakest a fearful riddle
I *will* not understand.

POL. Yet now as Fate
Approaches, and the Hours are breathing low,
The sands of Time are changed to golden grains,
And dazzle me, Baldazzar. Alas! alas!
I *cannot* die, having within my heart
So keen a relish for the beautiful
As hath been kindled within it. Methinks the air
Is balmier now than it was wont to be—
Rich melodies are floating in the winds—
A rarer loveliness bedecks the earth—
And with a holier luster the quiet moon
Sitteth in Heaven.—Hist! hist! thou canst not say
Thou hearest not *now*, Baldazzar?

BAL. Indeed I hear not.

POL. Not hear it!—listen now—listen!—the faintest
    sound
And yet the sweetest that ear ever heard!
A lady's voice!—and sorrow in the tone!
Baldazzar, it oppresses me like a spell!

Again!—again!—how solemnly it falls
Into my heart of hearts! that eloquent voice
Surely I never heard—yet it were well
Had I *but* heard it with its thrilling tones
In earlier days!

    Bal. I myself hear it now.
Be still!—the voice, if I mistake not greatly,
Proceeds from yonder lattice—which you may see
Very plainly through the window—it belongs,
Does it not? unto this palace of the Duke.
The singer is undoubtedly beneath
The roof of his Excellency—and perhaps
Is even that Alessandra of whom he spoke
As the betrothed of Castiglione,
His son and heir.

    Pol. Be still!—it comes again!

    Voice   "And is thy heart so strong
(*very faintly.*)   As for to leave me thus
             Who hath loved thee so long
             In wealth and wo among?
             And is thy heart so strong
             As for to leave me thus?
                  Say nay—say nay!"

    Bal. The song is English, and I oft have heard it
In merry England—never so plaintively—
Hist! hist! it comes again!

    Voice   "Is it so strong
(*more loudly.*)   As for to leave me thus
             Who hath loved thee so long
             In wealth and wo among?
             And is thy heart so strong
             As for to leave me thus?
                  Say nay—say nay!"

    Bal. 'Tis hushed and all is still!

    Pol. All *is not* still.

    Bal. Let us go down.

Pol. Go down, Baldazzar, go!

Bal. The hour is growing late—the Duke awaits us,—
Thy presence is expected in the hall
Below. What ails thee, Earl Politian?

Voice   "Who hath loved thee so long,
(*distinctly.*)   In wealth and wo among,
         And is thy heart so strong?
         Say nay—say nay!"

Bal. Let us descend!—'tis time. Politian, give
These fancies to the wind. Remember, pray,
Your bearing lately savored much of rudeness
Unto the Duke. Arouse thee! and remember!

Pol. Remember? I do. Lead on! I *do* remember. (*going.*)
Let us descend. Believe me I would give,
Freely would give the broad lands of my earldom
To look upon the face hidden by yon lattice—
"To gaze upon that veiled face, and hear
Once more that silent tongue."

Bal. Let me beg you, sir,
Descend with me—the Duke may be offended.
Let us go down, I pray you.

    (*Voice loudly.*) *Say nay!—say nay!*

Pol. (*aside.*) 'Tis strange!—'tis very strange—methought
   the voice
Chimed in with my desires and bade me stay!
         (*approaching the window.*)
Sweet voice! I heed thee, and will surely stay.
Now be this Fancy, by Heaven, or be it Fate,
Still will I not descend. Baldazzar, make
Apology unto the Duke for me;
I go not down tonight.

Bal. Your lordship's pleasure
Shall be attended to. Good night, Politian.

Pol. Good night, my friend, good night.

The gardens of a palace—Moonlight. Lalage and Politian.

LALAGE. And dost thou speak of love
To *me*, Politian?—dost thou speak of love
To Lalage?—ah wo—ah wo is me!
This mockery is most cruel—most cruel indeed!

POLITIAN. Weep not! oh, sob not thus!—thy bitter tears
Will madden me. Oh mourn not, Lalage—
Be comforted! I know—I know it all,
And *still* I speak of love. Look at me, brightest,
And beautiful Lalage!—turn here thine eyes!
Thou askest me if I could speak of love,
Knowing what I know, and seeing what I have seen.
Thou askest me that—and thus I answer thee—
Thus on my bended knee I answer thee. (*kneeling.*)
Sweet Lalage, *I love thee—love thee—love thee;*
Thro' good and ill—thro' weal and wo I *love thee.*
Not mother, with her first born on her knee,
Thrills with intenser love than I for thee.
Not on God's altar, in any time or clime,
Burned there a holier fire than burneth now
Within my spirit for *thee.* And do I love? (*arising.*)
Even for thy woes I love thee—even for thy woes—
Thy beauty and thy woes.

LAL. Alas, proud Earl,
Thou dost forget thyself, remembering me!
How, in thy father's halls, among the maidens
Pure and reproachless of thy princely line,
Could the dishonored Lalage abide?
Thy wife, and with a tainted memory—
My seared and blighted name, how would it tally
With the ancestral honors of thy house,
And with thy glory?

POL. Speak not to me of glory!

I hate—I loathe the name; I do abhor
The unsatisfactory and ideal thing.
Art thou not Lalage and I Politian?
Do I not love—art thou not beautiful—
What need we more? Ha! glory!—now speak not of it!
By all I hold most sacred and most solemn—
By all my wishes now—my fears hereafter—
By all I scorn on earth and hope in heaven—
There is no deed I would more glory in,
Than in thy cause to scoff at this same glory
And trample it under foot. What matters it—
What matters it, my fairest, and my best,
That we go down unhonored and forgotten
Into the dust—so we descend together.
Descend together—and then—and then perchance——
    Lal. Why dost thou pause, Politian?
    Pol. And then perchance
Arise together, Lalage, and roam
The starry and quiet dwellings of the blest,
And still——
    Lal. Why dost thou pause, Politian?
    Pol. And still *together—together.*
    Lal. Now Earl of Leicester!
Thou *lovest* me, and in my heart of hearts
I feel thou lovest me truly.
    Pol. Oh, Lalage! (*throwing himself upon his knee.*)
And lovest thou *me?*
    Lal. Hist! hush! within the gloom
Of yonder trees methought a figure past—
A spectral figure, solemn, and slow, and noiseless—
Like the grim shadow Conscience, solemn and noiseless.
              (*walks across and returns.*)
I was mistaken—'twas but a giant bough
Stirred by the autumn wind. Politian!
    Pol. My Lalage—my love! why art thou moved?
Why dost thou turn so pale? Not Conscience' self,

Far less a shadow which thou likenest to it,
Should shake the firm spirit thus. But the night wind
Is chilly—and these melancholy boughs
Throw over all things a gloom.
    LAL. Politian!
Thou speakest to me of love. Knowest thou the land
With which all tongues are busy—a land new found—
Miraculously found by one of Genoa—
A thousand leagues within the golden west?
A fairy land of flowers, and fruit, and sunshine,
And crystal lakes, and overarching forests,
And mountains, around whose towering summits the winds
Of Heaven untrammelled flow—which air to breathe
Is Happiness now, and will be Freedom hereafter
In days that are to come?
    POL. O, wilt thou—wilt thou
Fly to that Paradise—my Lalage, wilt thou
Fly thither with me? There Care shall be forgotten,
And Sorrow shall be no more, and Eros be all.
And life shall then be mine, for I will live
For thee, and in thine eyes—and thou shalt be
No more a mourner—but the radiant Joys
Shall wait upon thee, and the angel Hope
Attend thee ever; and I will kneel to thee
And worship thee, and call thee my beloved,
My own, my beautiful, my love, my wife,
My all;—oh, wilt thou—wilt thou, Lalage,
Fly thither with me?
    LAL. A deed is to be done—
Castiglione lives!
    POL. And he shall die! (*exit.*)
    LAL. (*after a pause.*) And—he shall—die!——alas!
Castiglione die? Who spoke the words?
Where am I?—what was it he said?—Politian!
Thou *art* not gone—thou art not *gone*, Politian!
I *feel* thou art not gone—yet dare not look.

Lest I behold thee not; thou *couldst* not go
With those words upon thy lips—O, speak to me!
And let me hear thy voice—one word—one word,
To say thou art not gone,—one little sentence,
To say how thou dost scorn—how thou dost hate
My womanly weakness. Ha! ha! thou *art* not gone—
O speak to me! I *knew* thou wouldst not go!
I knew thou wouldst not, couldst not, *durst* not go.
Villain, thou *art* not gone—thou mockest me!
And thus I clutch thee—thus!——He is gone, he is
        gone—
Gone—gone. Where am I?——'tis well—'tis very well!
So that the blade be keen—the blow be sure,
'Tis well, 'tis *very* well—alas! alas! (*exit.*)

v

The suburbs. Politian alone.
POLITIAN. This weakness grows upon me. I am faint,
And much I fear me ill—it will not do
To die ere I have lived!—Stay—stay thy hand,
O Azrael, yet awhile!—Prince of the Powers
Of Darkness and the Tomb, O pity me!
O pity me! let me not perish now,
In the budding of my Paradisal Hope!
Give me to live yet—yet a little while:
'Tis I who pray for life—I who so late
Demanded but to die!—what sayeth the Count?
                Enter Baldazzar.
BALDAZZAR. That knowing no cause of quarrel or of feud
Between the Earl Politian and himself,
He doth decline your cartel.
    POL. *What* didst thou say?
What answer was it you brought me, good Baldazzar?

With what excessive fragrance the zephyr comes
Laden from yonder bowers!—a fairer day,
Or one more worthy Italy, methinks
No mortal eyes have seen!—*what* said the Count?

BAL. That he, Castiglione, not being aware
Of any feud existing, or any cause
Of quarrel between your lordship and himself
Cannot accept the challenge.

POL. It is most true—
All this is very true. When saw you, sir,
When saw you now, Baldazzar, in the frigid
Ungenial Britain which we left so lately,
A heaven so calm as this—so utterly free
From the evil taint of clouds?—and he did *say?*

BAL. No more, my lord, than I have told you, sir:
The Count Castiglione will not fight,
Having no cause for quarrel.

POL. Now this is true—
All very true. Thou art my friend, Baldazzar,
And I have not forgotten it—thou'lt do me
A piece of service; wilt thou go back and say
Unto this man, that I, the Earl of Leicester,
Hold him a villain?—thus much, I prythee, say
Unto the Count—it is exceeding just
He should have cause for quarrel.

BAL. My lord!—my friend!——

POL. (*aside.*) 'Tis he—he comes himself! (*aloud.*) thou
    reasonest well.
I know what thou wouldst say—not send the message—
Well!—I will think of it—I will not send it.
Now prythee, leave me—hither doth come a person
With whom affairs of a most private nature
I would adjust.

BAL. I go—tomorrow we meet,
Do we not?—at the Vatican.

POL. At the Vatican. (*exit Bal.*)

Enter Castiglione.

Cas. The Earl of Leicester here!

Pol. I *am* the Earl of Leicester, and thou seest,
Dost thou not? that I am here.

Cas. My lord, some strange,
Some singular mistake—misunderstanding—
Hath without doubt arisen: thou hast been urged
Thereby, in heat of anger, to address
Some words most unaccountable, in writing,
To me, Castiglione; the bearer being
Baldazzar, Duke of Surrey. I am aware
Of nothing which might warrant thee in this thing,
Having given thee no offence. Ha!—am I right?
'Twas a mistake?—undoubtedly—we all
Do err at times.

Pol. Draw, villain, and prate no more!

Cas. Ha!—draw?—and villain? have at thee then at
    once,
Proud Earl! (*draws.*)

Pol. (*drawing.*) Thus to the expiatory tomb,
Untimely sepulcher, I do devote thee
In the name of Lalage!

Cas. (*letting fall his sword and recoiling to the extremity of
    the stage.*)
Of Lalage!
Hold off—thy sacred hand!—avaunt I say!
Avaunt—I will not fight thee—indeed I dare not.

Pol. Thou wilt not fight with me didst say, Sir Count?
Shall I be baffled thus?—now this is well;
Didst say thou *darest* not? Ha!

Cas. I dare not—dare not—
Hold off thy hand—with that beloved name
So fresh upon thy lips I will not fight thee—
I cannot—dare not.

Pol. Now by my halidom
I do believe thee!—coward, I do believe thee!

CAS. Ha!—coward!—this may not be!
  (*clutches his sword and staggers towards Politian,
    but his purpose is changed before reaching him,
    and he falls upon his knee at the feet of the Earl.*)
                 Alas ! my lord,
It is—it is—most true. In such a cause
I am the veriest coward. O pity me!
  POL. (*greatly softened.*) Alas!—I do—indeed I pity thee.
  CAS. And Lalage——
  POL. *Scoundrel!—arise and die!*
  CAS. It needeth not be—thus—thus—O let me die
Thus on my bended knee. It were most fitting
That in this deep humiliation I perish.
For in the fight I will not raise a hand
Against thee, Earl of Leicester. Strike thou home—
    (*baring his bosom.*)
Here is no let or hindrance to thy weapon—
Strike home. I *will not* fight thee.
  POL. Now s' Death and Hell!
Am I not—am I not sorely—grievously tempted
To take thee at thy word? But mark me, sir!
Think not to fly me thus. Do thou prepare
For public insult in the streets—before
The eyes of the citizens. I'll follow thee—
Like an avenging spirit I'll follow thee
Even unto death. Before those whom thou lovest—
Before all Rome I'll taunt thee, villain,—I'll taunt thee,
Dost hear? with *cowardice*—thou *wilt not* fight me?
Thou liest! thou *shalt!* (*exit.*)
  CAS. Now this indeed is just!
Most righteous, and most just, avenging Heaven!